中国人的40年

CHANGES IN CHINESE LIFE IN 40 YEARS

中国画报出版社 编
China Pictorial Press

中国画报出版社·北京
China Pictorial Press · Beijing

图书在版编目（CIP）数据

中国人的40年：汉英对照 / 中国画报出版社编. —
北京：中国画报出版社, 2018.12
　ISBN 978-7-5146-1701-6

Ⅰ. ①中… Ⅱ. ①中… Ⅲ. ①改革开放—成就—中国
—摄影集 Ⅳ. ①D619-64

中国版本图书馆CIP数据核字(2018)第275356号

中国人的40年（中英文）

中国画报出版社　编

责任编辑：刘晓雪
英文编辑：朱露茜
图片编辑：刘晓雪　朱露茜　陈　曦　王丽艳　闻礼华
英文翻译：钱　清
英文改稿：Geoffrey Murry
英文审定：王国振
封面设计：郑建军
内文设计：刘　凤　郑建军
责任印制：焦　洋

出版发行：中国画报出版社
地　　址：中国北京市海淀区车公庄西路33号　邮编：100048
发 行 部：010-68469781　010-68414683（传真）
总编室兼传真：010-88417359　版权部：010-88417359

开　本：16开（889mm×1194mm）
印　张：18.75
字　数：150千字
版　次：2018年12月第1版　2018年12月第1次印刷
印　刷：捷鹰印刷（天津）有限公司
书　号：ISBN 978-7-5146-1701-6
定　价：298.00元

前　言

　　2018年，是中国改革开放40周年。1978年12月，中国共产党第十一届中央委员会第三次全体会议在北京举行，会议做出了实行改革开放的重大决策，党和国家工作重心转移到经济建设上来，开启了"改革开放"的新篇章。

　　40年间，中国取得了举世瞩目的伟大成就，从综合国力到社会面貌，从文化建设到日常生活，特别是中国的百姓生活发生了翻天覆地的变化。百姓的衣着从"蓝黑灰"走向 "个性化"；饮食从"解决温饱"走向"吃出健康"；住房从"蜗居"走向"广厦"；出行方式从"单一"走向"多元"；生活用品从传统的"三大件"到如今层出不穷的高科技产品；教育发展日新月异，教育系统日臻完善，国民受教育程度大大提高；科技发展势头迅猛，多个领域由赶超世界先进水平，发展为引领发展趋势……

　　40年，280张照片，上百位摄影师用手中的相机记录了百姓生活的点点滴滴，见证了神州大地上发生的沧桑巨变。

　　历史照见未来，让我们跟随摄影师的镜头，重温历史，珍惜当下，憧憬未来……

Preface

The year 2018 marks the 40th anniversary of China's reform and opening up. In late December 1978, the Third Plenary Session of the 11th Central Committee of the Communist Party of China was held in Beijing. It made a major decision to introduce the innovative program of reform and opening up in a shift of focus in State work to economic construction.

Over the past 40 years, China has made great achievements that have attracted worldwide attention. Great changes have taken place in terms of comprehensive national strength as well as social outlook, from cultural construction to various aspects in the daily life of the Chinese people. The world was marvelous to see changes taking place in China - changes from everyone wearing the same drab work clothes (earning the sobriquet in the West of "blue ants") to clothes with a distinct individual "personality"; from "managing to solve food shortages" to "eating for health"; from living in "humble (cramped) rooms" to possessing "decent apartments"; from travelling in a "single way" to a "pluralistic " approach; and from "three basic needs for the household" (radio, sewing machine and a bicycle) to ownership of a wide range of high-tech products. During the 40-year period, China has seen earthshaking changes in education, systemic improvements occurring with each passing day, and all Chinese increasingly receiving quality education; science and technology developing apace, with many fields developing from "catching up with the world's advanced level" to leading the development trend....

With 280 photographs taken by up to 100 photographers, our pictorial is aimed at showing readers the momentous changes that have taken place in various aspects of life in China.

Let's follow the progress through photographer's lens to review history, cherish the present, and look forward to the future...

第一章 衣   001
Chapter I Clothing   001

第二章 食   043
Chapter II Food   043

第三章 住   085
Chapter III Housing   085

第四章 行   127
Chapter IV Travel   127

第五章 用   169
Chapter V Articles for Daily Use   169

第六章 教育   211
Chapter VI Education   211

第七章 科技   253
Chapter VII Science and Technology   253

衣

Chapter I Clothing

第一章

中国人的40年
CHANGES IN CHINESE LIFE IN 40 YEARS

1979 安徽嘉山,司巷公社岗北队社员添置了新衣。二十世纪七十年代,在几亿中国人的衣柜里,绿、蓝、黑、灰等几种颜色的衣服占据了绝对的"统治地位"

Members of the Gangbei Production Brigade of the Sixiang People's Commune in Jiashan, Anhui Province, happy to have new clothes. In the 1970s, hundreds of millions of Chinese people wore clothes mainly of a somber hue, such as blue, black, grey and perhaps dark green.

1980 福建厦门，第四塑料厂的工人在加工凉拖鞋，这是当时流行的凉拖鞋样式

In Xiamen, Fujian Province, workers at the 4th Plastic Factory process sandals, much in demand around 1980.

1981 上海，一位妈妈在给孩子试穿新衣。当时，手工缝制的衣服开始出现个性化的设计，服装的颜色也越来越鲜艳
A mother tries new dress on her child in Shanghai in 1981. At that time, hand-made clothes were beginning to appear with personalized designs, and they also became more colorful.

1982 北京百货大楼里,人们在挑选布匹做衣服。二十世纪八十年代,买布料自制服装仍是主流

Consumers buy cloth to make their own clothes at the Beijing Department Store. In the 1980s, homemade clothing was still very common.

1983 北京王府井大街上的中国照相馆,一对新人穿着时兴的结婚礼服喜留佳影
Taking wedding pictures while donning fashionable wedding dresses at the Chinese Photo Gallery on Wangfujing Street in the center of Beijing.

1984 / 河北玉田，一家人穿着朴素的衣服拍摄全家福

Portrait of a family posing in very simple clothes in Yutian, Hebei Province.

1985 北京动物园门前，穿着喇叭裤，披着军大衣的时髦青年。二十世纪八十年代初期，喇叭裤、军大衣一度是时尚青年最喜爱的衣服

Young people wearing bell bottoms and military-style overcoats in front of Beijing Zoo. In the early 1980s, such clothing was the favorites of the fashionable young.

衣 Clothing | 009

1986 北京，一位老人和他穿西服的孙子。二十世纪八十年代，全国掀起"西装潮"，中山装、军便装逐渐退出时装舞台
An old man and his grandson in Western suits. In the 1980s, Chinese tunic suits and military-style clothing gradually withdrew from the fashion stage, making way for Western apparel.

1987 | 广东广州,在第九届日用工业品交流会上展示的当时被认为"新颖时尚"的服装
Newly designed fashions are exhibited at the 9th Commodities Fair for Manufactured Goods for Daily Use in Guangzhou, Guangdong Province,.

衣 Clothing | 011

1988

北京的春天虽然时有寒意，但爱美的姑娘们迫不及待地穿上了健美裤、宽松套裙等流行的春装
Although Spring is still cold in North China, girls wear form-fitting pants, loose overskirts and other high fashion garments.

1989 上海，一对新人在婚宴开始之前穿着新婚礼服在酒店门口迎候亲友
Newlyweds greet guests attending their wedding banquet at a hotel entrance in Shanghai.

1990 / 海南三亚,年轻女孩的穿着反映了当时的潮流

The dress of young girls in Sanya, Hainan Province represents what is in fashion in the country when the photograph was taken.

1991 上海，穿着时尚服装的女性。二十世纪九十年代初期，中国的服装市场开始猛追世界潮流，时逢西方女装流行宽肩，于是中国都市女性的大衣、套装、毛衣，甚至衬衫、连衣裙都添加了海绵垫肩

Women in fashionable clothes. In the early 1990s, China's clothing market finally began to catch up with world trends. At that time, women's clothing with wide shoulders was in fashion in the West, so, sponge shoulder pads were added to Chinese urban women's coats, suits, sweaters, and even shirts and dresses.

1992 江苏南京，模特向顾客展示牛仔系列时装。二十世纪九十年代初期，中国本土牛仔服生产厂家逐渐增多，牛仔服作为一种时尚穿着被大众所接受

Models showing a range of cowboy fashion in Nanjing, Jiangsu Province. In the early 1990s, jeans manufacturers flourished in China as a result of growing popularity.

1993 辽宁沈阳的第一家婚纱影楼前,模特穿着当时流行的婚纱进行展示
Models display popular wedding dresses before the First Wedding Photo Studio in Shenyang, Liaoning Province.

1994 云南昆明，身着当时流行的紧身裤的妇女。继二十世纪八十年代流行的健美裤之后，这种五分式的紧身裤开始在全国范围内流行

Women wearing hip-hugging pants then in vogue in Kunming, Yunnan Province. Following bodybuilding pants becoming fashionable in China in the 1980s, tight pants begin to gain popularity in the country.

1995 北京，穿着各式棉服的大学生在什刹海滑冰

College students dressed in all kinds of winter clothes skate in Shichahai, a famous lake in central Beijing.

衣 Clothing | 019

1996 / 山西，身着皮夹克的姑娘们。二十世纪九十年代初期，全国各地都出现了皮衣热。在这一年，皮装消费达到了巅峰
Girls in leather jackets. In the early 1990s, fur-lined leather jackets gained popularity throughout China, with sales reaching a record high.

1997 首届中国服装设计博览会成功举办，这是中国时装设计界第一次集体发声，中国时尚产业由此进入新阶段。图为著名青年设计师马羚在博览会上展示她的服装作品

With the success of the First China Fashion Design Fair in the year, China's fashion industry enters a new stage of development. The picture shows a famous young designer, Ma Ling, displaying her clothes at the fair.

1998 重庆，首届汽车摩托模特大赛的决赛现场。汽车模特是随着汽车工业的发展而出现的新兴职业
A shot of the First Automobile and Motorcycle Motor Racing Models Competition Final in Chongqing. The emergence of various models revealed the fast development of the automobile industry.

1999 各式各样的儿童服装越来越个性化。二十世纪九十年代末期，中国年产服装近两百亿件，花色繁多，门类齐全
With garments becoming increasingly individualized in colors and design, China produced nearly 20 billion garments reflecting that trend.

2000

哈尔滨,等待面试的模特。二十世纪九十年代末期,从模特业进入影视娱乐业的例子比比皆是,早几年入行并已功成名就的胡兵、瞿颖就是典型的例子。这使得更多怀揣演艺梦想的青年加入模特大军

Models waiting for interview in Harbin, Heilongjiang Province in 2000. In the late 1990s, models began entering the film and television entertainment industry. Cases in point include girls such as Hu Bing and Qu Ying, who had become household names a few years earlier. More young people with artistic dreams yearn to join the model army.

2001

广东深圳,着装开放的年轻人。二十世纪九十年代末期,人们的物质生活越来越丰富,思想观念更为开放,穿衣打扮讲求个性和多变,很难用一种款式或色彩来概括时尚潮流,强调个性、不追逐流行本身也成为一种时尚 Young people dressed fashionably in the Shenzhen Special Economic Zone, Guangdong Province. In the late 1990s, the Chinese people enjoy a better quality-life and become increasingly open-minded in ideology. They chase fashion and emphasize changing individuality in dress.

2002

江苏南京，孩子穿唐装过年。在 2001 年亚太经合组织（APEC）第九次领导人非正式会议期间，二十位中外领导人在上海穿着唐装亮相后，全国刮起了"复古风"，开始流行各式唐装

Children wearing traditional Chinese garments called Tang Dynasty costumes for the Chinese New Year celebration in Nanjing, Jiangsu Province. When the CCTV news showed the Chinese and foreign leaders wearing Tang Dynasty costumes at the APEC Meeting in 2001, such clothing became fashionable.

2003

江苏南京，穿着吊带背心、短袖衫等流行服装的女孩。随着时代发展，人们的穿着打扮愈发个性化，吊带背心、超短裙、字母短袖衫等时尚服装逐渐为人们所接受
Girls wearing fashionable clothes such as camisoles and T-shirts in Nanjing, Jiangsu Province. With fast economic development, people's dress became increasingly personalized, and such aspects as suspender belts, miniskirts and T-shirts became common sights.

衣 Clothing | 027

2004

福建福州，身着前卫流行服装的年轻人。在二十一世纪初期，中国人对服饰诉求的最高境界是穿出个性，最好做到独一无二。服装的主要作用已经不再是御寒，而是一种个性魅力的体现

Young people wearing avant-garde fashions in Fuzhou, Fujian Province. In the early 21st Century, many Chinese begin seeking clothing with individualized design. They no longer wore clothes to keep out the cold; instead, they began wearing them to show individual charm.

2005 北京，王府井百货大楼，模特在广场前展示新款羽绒服。与以往传统的冬装棉大衣和厚重的羽绒服相比，更轻薄且更具时装概念的羽绒服逐渐成为消费者新宠

Fashion models exhibiting new-style duck down-padded garments at Department Store Square on Wangfujing Street, the famous shipping street of central Beijing. Compared with old-style ones that were heavier, the new styles attracted consumers because of being lighter and more fashionable in style.

衣 Clothing | 029

2006 广东广州，留着新潮发型、穿着各异的年轻女孩们在自拍留念。当时，年轻人开始选择个性化的颜色挑染头发，不再局限于黄色、棕色等常见发色

Girls wearing fashionable hairstyles and clothes take self-portraits in Guangzhou, Guangdong Province. In the first decade of the new century, some young people dye their hair in various colors in pursuit of fashion.

2007 / 北京，东方新天地商场，路人走过一间国际名牌时装专卖店。同一时期，各地开始出现高端购物场所以满足人们日益增长的购物需求

People walking in front of an international brand fashion store at the Dongfang Xintiandi Plaza in Beijing. The period saw the emergence of stores exclusively for high-end shopping malls.

2008 / 一场科技·时尚服装表演在北京服装学院进行，服饰与科技等其他元素结合得越来越紧密
Science and Technology - Fashion Show being staged at the Beijing Institute of Fashion. Clothing is increasingly integrated with elements of science and technology.

2009 北京怀柔，一个社区的居民在制作"珠绣"服装，这种中国民族服饰远销澳大利亚、印度、泰国等国家。随着中国综合国力和国际地位的不断提升，具有中国特色的传统服饰开始走向世界，中国服装在全球受到瞩目和尊重

People living in a residential quarter in Huairou, Beijing, make "beaded embroidery" clothes in 2009 for export to Australia, India, Thailand and other countries. With the continuous improvement of China's comprehensive national strength and international status, traditional clothing with Chinese characteristics has begun to penetrate more international markets, attracting worldwide attention and respect.

衣 Clothing | *033*

2010

浙江杭州,银泰武林店广场上,百余名身穿时尚服装的年轻人手拿自己的靓照,向人们大胆展示自己的风采

In front of the Wulin Square Yintai in Hangzhou, Zhejiang Province, some 100 young people, wearing fashionable clothes, show their own beautiful photos to people.

2011 浙江嘉兴,凌公塘公园,一群年轻人身着艳丽的"二次元"服装与一对拍摄婚纱照的新人擦肩而过。穿着像动漫角色一样夸张的服装,染着五颜六色的头发……在大多数人眼里,看起来有些稀奇古怪的二次元元素,成为当时一些年轻人的追求

A group of young people, wearing strange clothes displaying "quadratic elements", pass by a couple taking wedding photos at Linggongtang Park, Jiaxing, Zhejiang Province in 2011. They look like characters out of anime works, wearing exaggerated costumes and with dyed hair of different colors. These quadratic elements, however, are just what some young people were beginning to pursue.

2012

上海，闸北区丝绸贸易总公司门前，身着丝绸旗袍的模特们正在拍摄合影，一位穿着朴素的骑车人从镜头前穿过

In front of Zhabei District Silk Trade Corporation in Shanghai, a group of models wearing silk cheongsam pose for photos as a cyclist passes before the camera.

2013 / 北京，新世界百货商场里琳琅满目的服装
A dazzling variety of fashions at the New World Department Store in 2013.

衣 Clothing | 037

2014 / 北京，人们穿着复古服装参加一场骑行活动。近年来，衣服的款式越来越多样化、多元化，复古风便是其中一种流行的服饰风格

People in retro costumes participate in a riding activity in Beijing in 2014. In recent years, clothing styles have become more and more diversified, and retro style is one of the popular styles.

2015 湖北武汉,十六位女企业家变身模特,身着为自己量身定制的服装登台。越来越多的消费者开始追求衣着的个性化与私人化,高级服装定制兴起

A fashion show is going on in Wuhan, Hubei Province. The 16 models on display are female entrepreneurs wearing custom-made clothes at a time when more and more consumers begin to pursue the individuation and privatization of clothing.

2016 / 参加法国巴黎"2016维多利亚的秘密"时装秀(简称"维密秀")的四位中国模特
Four Chinese models attending the Victoria's Secret Fashion Show 2016 in Paris, France.

2017 江苏南京，顾客正在体验"虚拟试衣镜"，不用脱衣也能换装，高科技进入服装零售业

Customers experiencing a "virtual fitting mirror" in Nanjing, Jiangsu Province in 2017. With such a mirror, customers can try on clothes without any disrobing, showing how high-tech has moved into apparel retailing.

衣 Clothing | 041

2018 / 一位全职妈妈将自己设计的童装给女儿穿上，这位妈妈自己创业，开网店设计、出售童装。科技的发展正在快速改变中国人的着装生活

A full-time mother dresses her daughter in new clothes she has designed. The young mother had launched an online store to design and sell children's clothes. Technology has drastically changed Chinese people's dress sense.

食

Chapter II Food

第二章

中国人的 40 年
CHANGES IN CHINESE LIFE IN 40 YEARS

1979 / 福建福州，一家粮店推出流动售卖服务
A grain store launches a mobile sales vehicle service in Fuzhou, Fujian Province.

1980 / 北京，内地第一家个体饭馆"悦宾"开业。当时，美国合众社对悦宾做了报道，全世界都知道了这家胡同里的饭馆
When Yuebin, the first privately-owned restaurant in the Chinese mainland, opened for business, United Press International of the United States published a report on this small restaurant in a Beijing hutong.

1981 / 北京，前门路边的大碗茶
Big-bowl tea sold at Qianmen, in the Tian'anmen Square area.

1982 上海，杨浦区抚顺路，四位女青年在自家门口摆摊，卖起了上海人喜欢吃的大饼、油条。这是上海较早的"个体户"
Four young women set up stalls at Fushun Road in Yangpu District, Shanghai, selling roasted cakes and deep-fried dough sticks, much loved by local people. They were among the first group of "self-employed people" in the city.

1983 四川，婆媳二人在为全家准备丰盛的午餐

Mother-in-law and daughter-in-law in Sichuan preparing for a sumptuous family lunch.

1984 — 北京,市民在街头抢购冬储大白菜。在那个年代,整整一个冬季,白菜是全北京乃至北方各地城市居民的当家菜
Beijing residents rushing to buy cabbages to tide over freezing winter. This was a typical scene in North China in the last century.

1985 安徽滁县，集市上的肥猪肉颇受欢迎。在二十世纪七八十年代，许多家庭会把肥肉熬成猪油，用来炒素菜。在五零后、六零后的记忆中，熬猪油剩下的油渣堪称天下美味

Fat pork enjoys good sale in Chuxian County, Anhui Province in the 1970s and 1980s. Many families cooked fat to produce lard for cooking vegetables. In the memory of people, born in the 1950s and 1960s, dregs of fat were much-coveted food.

1986 / 北京，北冰洋汽水曾一度牢牢占据了京城冷饮领域的"大哥"位置
Arctic soda firmly occupies a good share of the cold drink market in Beijing.

1987 北京，内地首家"洋快餐"——中美合资经营的"北京美国肯德基家乡鸡快餐厅"开始试营业

Beijing Kentucky Fried Chicken Restaurant, a joint venture between China and the United States, opened for trial operation on the mainland in 1987.

食 Food | 053

1988 / 贵州六盘水，市民最后一次排队领取肉票。1989年1月起，全国取消"肉票"制度
People in Liupanshui, Guizhou Province, queue in 1988 to get their last meat coupons, as meat would be sold freely in whole country the following year.

1989 / 上海,在推行菜场经营市场化后,最大的受惠者是老百姓。图为农贸市场里百姓在挑选品种丰富的各类蔬菜
Consumers are the biggest beneficiaries in the marketization of vegetable sales rights. Picture shows a rural fair in Shanghai.

食 Food | 055

1990 / 广东深圳，内地第一家麦当劳餐厅在解放路光华楼西华宫正式开业

In 1990, McDonald's opens its first restaurant in the mainland at Xihua Palace, Guanghua Building, Jiefang Road in Shenzhen, Guangdong Province.

1991 春节前夕,辽宁昌图,农贸市场上芹菜、西红柿等非应季菜随处可见,富裕起来的农民冬季吃菜不再以萝卜、白菜为主 Although in deep winter on the eve of the Chinese New Year, non-seasonal vegetables such as celery and tomatoes are available in rural markets in Changtu County, Liaoning Province. Farmers riding the reform tide to affluence were not satisfied any longer with radishes and Chinese cabbages that they used to have in winter.

1992 山西忻州，宁武县城居民家里，主人正忙活着制作过元宵节的各种传统食物
Making traditional food for the Lantern Festival at home in Ningwu County, Xinzhou City, Shanxi Province.

1993 浙江温州，一家餐馆的服务员将客户电话预定的饭菜送到客户家中。这是改革开放后内地早期的餐馆外卖服务
Restaurant waiters deliver food to diners who have ordered take-out dishes by telephone in Wenzhou—the earliest take-out service in the city in Zhejiang Province.

1994 江苏扬州,街头流动小吃摊
Street mobile food stalls in Yangzhou, Jiangsu Province.

1995 中国北方，农村百姓坐在炕上吃火锅。此时的菜品较之过去丰富了很多，多样的农副产品已经摆上了餐桌
Rural families love to sit and eat hot pot around a table on the *kang* (heatable brick bed) in winter during the 1990's. Compared to the past, nowadays the table is loaded with varieties of agricultural and sideline products.

食 Food | 061

1996 / 湖南湘西土家族苗族自治州，吉首农贸市场肉食摊点
A shot of meat stalls at a Jishou rural market in the Xiangxi Tujia and Miao Ethnic Groups Autonomous Prefecture in Hunan Province.

1997 北京首家"洋超市"——"中贸联万客隆"开业。此后,外资超市逐渐进入中国市场
CTA Makro, first Sino-foreign supermarket in Beijing, opens. Since then, "foreign supermarkets" gradually entered the Chinese market in large numbers.

1998 北京，庙会上的老字号。人们生活富裕了，菜肴的种类丰富了，但是在传统的节日里，人们仍然会选择品尝传统食物
Old and famous shops at a temple fair in Beijing. With improvement in living conditions, people eat better. However, people continue to love the old foods during traditional festive days.

1999 成都，超市里包装精美、品种繁多的主副食品让人挑花了眼

A shot of a supermarkets in Chengdu, Sichuan Province, which supply a dazzling variety of staple and non-staple foods.

食 Food | 065

2000 / 安徽繁昌,荻港、孙村等乡镇纷纷建起了小型自选商店
Supermarkets appear even in small towns in Fanchang, Anhui Province, such as Digang and Suncun.

2001 / 福建福州，仓储式超市频频开业，去仓储超市购物改变了福州人传统的购物习惯
Warehouse supermarkets appears one after the other in Fuzhou, Fujian Province. This changes the shopping habits of local people.

2002 / 北京,中心使馆区内的三里屯酒吧街。二十世纪八十年代末期,毗邻使馆区的三里屯是北京最早出现的酒吧群落,只有老外是那里的常客。如今,泡吧已成为北京夜生活的一种形式

The Sanlitun Bar Street in the central embassy area in Beijing. In the late 1980s, the street was the earliest bar community in Beijing, but frequented only by foreigners. Nowadays, they are now very much part of the local social scene.

2003

北京，澳大利亚游客在前门全聚德老店品尝烤鸭。中国美食越来越受到国际友人的欢迎

Australian tourists eating roast duck at Qianmen Restaurant in Qianmen, central Beijing. Chinese cuisine is becoming ever more popular with international friends.

2004 江苏南京,市民在白马公园选购绿色生态农产品。人们越来越关注食品的安全问题

People buy green ecological products in Baima Park in Nanjing, Jiangsu Province. People pay more and more attention to food safety.

2005 / 重庆,市民正围坐在"天下第一大火锅"前享受着美食
No.1 Hot Pot Restaurant in the World in Chongqing Municipality directly under the Central Government.

2006

山东沾化，古城镇丁范村的老人正忙着和面捏制当地特色面食，迎接新春佳节。虽然物质生活越来越丰富，但是当地居民仍然保留着在传统节日中的饮食习俗

Seniors in Dingfan Village, Zhanhua, Shandong Province, make local specialty pasta to welcome the Chinese New Year. Life is increasingly good, but locals still retain traditional festival dietary customs.

2007 / 天津，来自全国十二个省市的三百余种中华名小吃亮相天津食品街，这是商家展示的超大月饼。中国人热爱美食，随着物质生活越来越丰富，人们开始追求饮食的个性化

More than 300 kinds of famous Chinese snacks from 12 provinces and municipalities on offer at the Food Street in Tianjin. Here a huge moon cake is displayed. With life increasingly getting better, consumers begin to pursue dietary individualization.

食 Food | 073

2008 / 浙江泰顺，该地区延续千年的百家宴传统
Hundred Family Banquet in Taishun County, Zhejiang Province. This tradition has been going on for some 1,000 years.

2009 / 四川南充,滨江美食文化周暨迎春购物月活动拉开序幕。此时,越来越多的餐饮商家打起文化牌,传统餐饮已经不仅仅可以饱口福,更被当作一种文化进行传播和推广

Binjiang Food Culture Week and Spring Festival Shopping Month opens in Nanchong, Sichuan Province. More and more restaurants offer traditional food as a way of promoting local culture.

2010 / 重庆，迎春新年名宴美食展在观音桥广场举行，各美食企业制作数十台年饭名宴进行展出并接受年夜饭预订。越来越多的家庭选择在饭店吃年夜饭

The Spring Festival Famous Banquet Food Exhibition opens at Guanyin Bridge Square in Chongqing. Dozens of famous Chinese New Year's Eve banquets are available for local people to make a reservation. On Chinese New Year's Eve, a happy moment for a family reunion, more and more people love to dine out.

2011 北京,二十辆外观新颖、干净整洁的早餐车出现在国贸地区街头
Twenty clean and tidy breakfast vehicles start business at the China World Trade Center in Beijing's CBD area.

2012

四川成都,一家怀旧主题咖啡厅。咖啡已经成为人们喜爱的日常饮品,咖啡厅也成为人们的社交、休闲场所
A nostalgia cafe in Chengdu, Sichuan Province. Coffee has become a favorite daily drink, and coffee bars have become places for people to socialize and relax.

2013 / 江苏南京,"南京大牌档"店内古朴整洁,恍如清末民初的酒楼茶馆

A simple, neatly-furnished snack restaurant in Nanjing, Jiangsu Province. It looks like a tea house in the late Qing Dynasty (1644-1911) and the early Republic of China (1912-1949).

2014 安徽合肥,首家机器人主题餐厅开门迎客,由机器人"大厨"和"跑堂"为顾客提供服务
This restaurant in Hefei, Anhui Province has robots who greet, cook and serve diners.

2015 山东东营，利津县第三实验幼儿园举行"快乐自助餐"活动
Happy Buffet held at the 3rd Experimental Kindergarten in Lijin County, Dongying, Shandong Province.

食 Food | 081

2016 北京，用餐软件"回家吃饭"，让厌倦了在饭馆吃饭的人们，上门或在自家就能吃到附近的美食达人们在家中制作的饭菜

Dining software called Home-Cook makes it possible for those who are tired of eating in crowded restaurants to eat meals made at home or in nearby gourmet outlets.

2017 重庆江北区，首创鸿恩店附近一外卖配送点，点外卖成为中国人吃饭的新选择
A take-out food distribution center near Hongen Store in Jiangbei District, Chongqing. Ordering food online has become a new choice for Chinese diners.

2018

上海,全球首家"X-24h 智慧便利店"正式落户地铁人民广场站内。这是一家以科技为核心驱动力的新概念便利店,为消费者提供了一套全新的鲜食现制现售解决方案

Shanghai's first X-24h Smart Convenience Store opened at the Subway People's Square. This is a new convenience store providing consumers with a new set of ready-made fresh food solutions.

住

Chapter III Housing

第三章

中国人的 40 年
CHANGES IN CHINESE LIFE IN 40 YEARS

1979 广东梅州，春节期间的普通民居
Ordinary residence during the Chinese New Year in Meizhou, Guangdong Province.

住 Housing | 087

1980 上海，卢湾区顺昌街道老式石库门房子里，三户居民合用一间不足七平方米的厨房

Three families share the same kitchen measuring less than seven square meters in an old-fashioned Shikumen house on Shunchang Street, Luwan District, Shanghai.

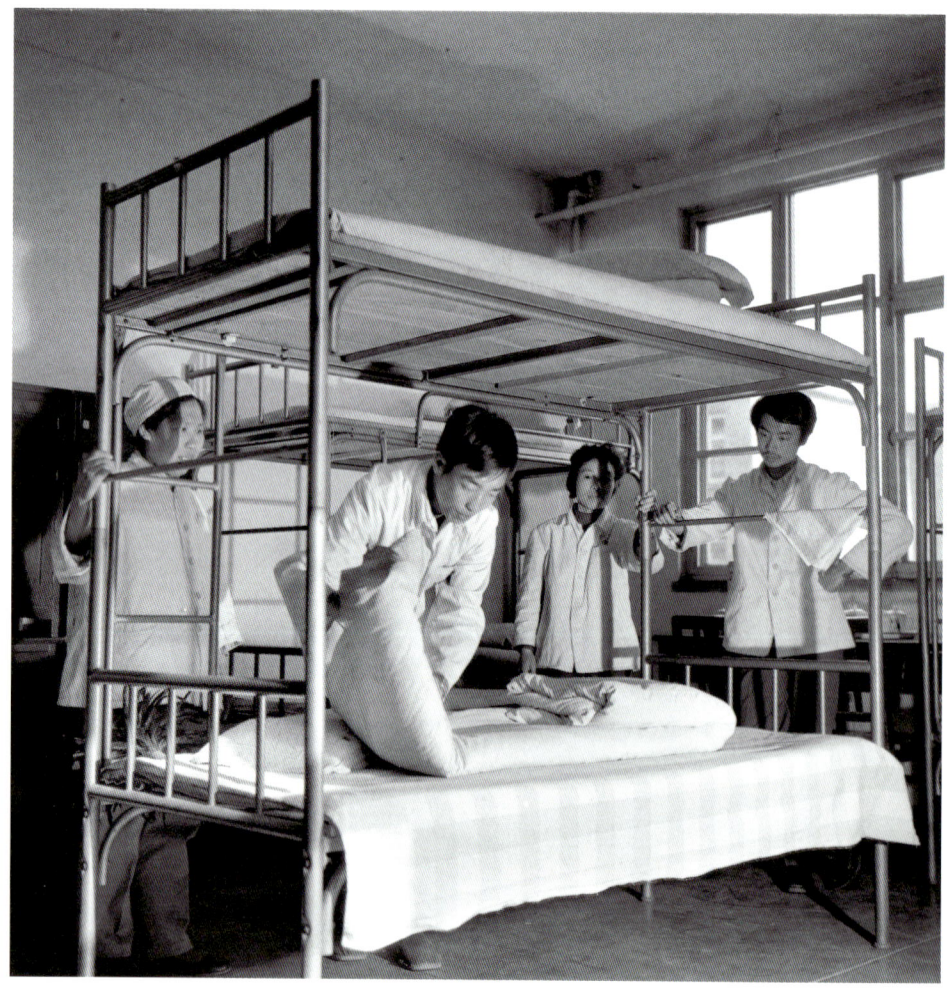

1981 / 北京，崇文门第二旅馆，很像"集体宿舍"
The No.2 Hostel in Chongwen, Beijing, is very much like a "dormitory".

1982 / 上海，卢湾区淡水路换房市场。当时实行分房制度，产权为国有。为了缓解住房困难，上海市民自发形成了包括卢湾区淡水路、徐汇区跳水池、虹口区昆山花园等在内的一批自由换房市场

Housing Exchange Market at Danshui Road, Luwan District, Shanghai. In the era of the planned economy, a housing distribution system was implemented, and the government owned the property rights. In order to alleviate housing difficulties, Shanghai citizens spontaneously formed a number of free housing exchange markets, including those at Danshui Road in Luwan District, Tiaoshuichi in Xuhui District and Kunshan Garden in Hongkou District.

1983 / 上海，一对新婚夫妻喜气洋洋地迁入"鸳鸯楼"。普陀区当时新建的第一幢结婚旅馆——"鸳鸯楼"，可作为晚婚青年结婚的过渡房屋

A newly-married couple happily move into Mandarin Duck Tower, newly-built by the Putuo District Real Estate Bureau in Shanghai, as a transitional housing arrangement for couples who had been postponing their marriage due to having no home.

1984 江苏江阴，华西村农民住宅中的西式客厅
Western-style living room of a farmer's residence in Huaxi Village, Jiangyin, Jiangsu Province.

1985 / 广东深圳,女工宿舍。在二十世纪八十年代末、九十年代初期,全国流行这样一句话:"东西南北中,发财到广东。"那个时候,越来越多的农村青年到大城市寻求新的发展机会

A women's dormitory in Shenzhen, Guangdong Province. In the late 1980s and the early 1990s, a popular saying across the country declared: "Want to make money? Go to Guangdong Province." This inspired many rural young people to migrate to work in Shenzhen and other big cities in the prospering southern region.

1986 广东，贫困山区一户农民凭着祖传的手艺富裕起来，并盖了新房

An impoverished family in Guangdong gather in the new house they have built with money earned using their own traditional ancestral skills.

1987 / 北京，白塔寺附近的民居
Residences in a hutong (lane) nearby White Dagoba Temple in Xicheng District of Beijing.

1988 上海，吴淞区摘牌拆迁，该区与宝山县合并为宝山区
In Shanghai, Wusong District and Baoshan County form the Baoshan District.

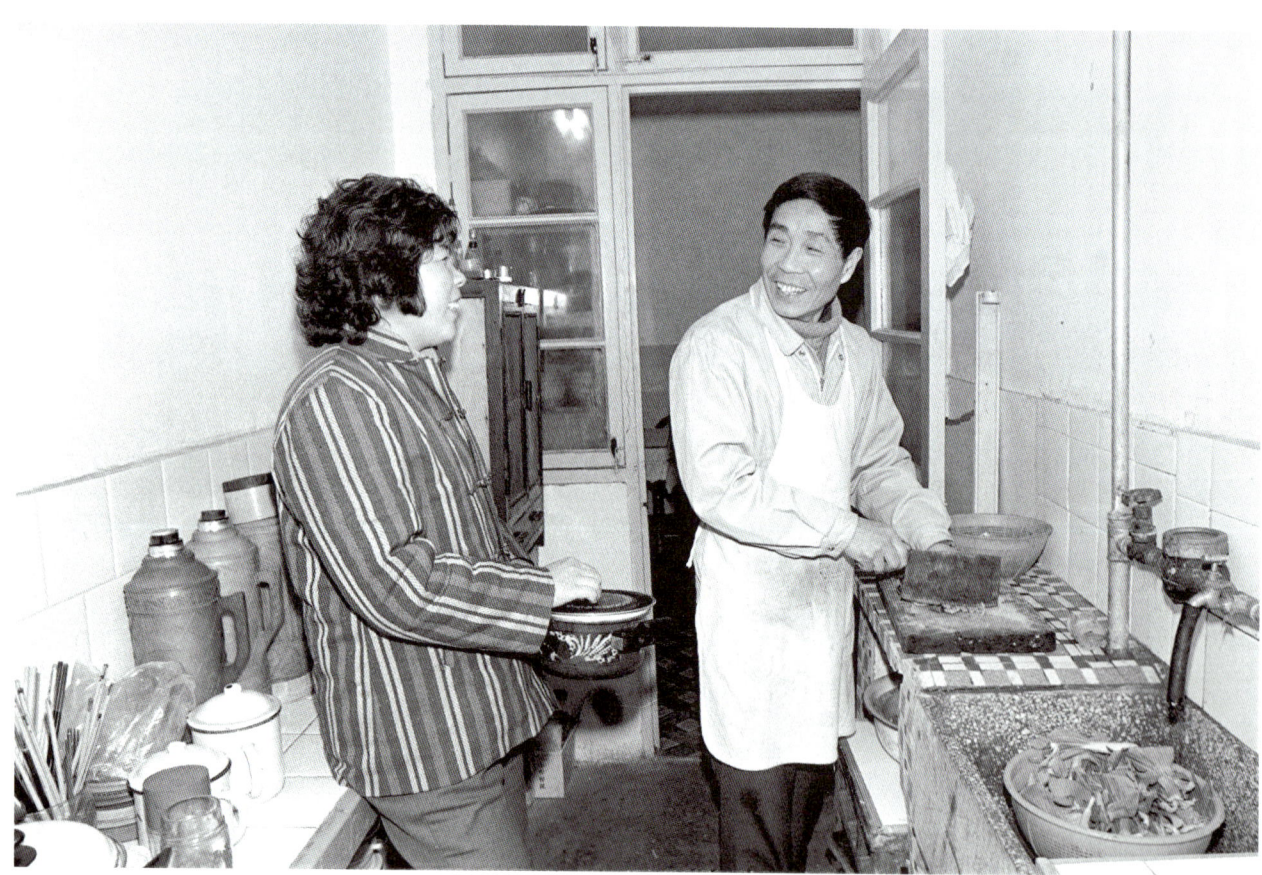

1989 / 安徽，蚌埠玻璃厂老工人沈业求（右）在个人集资建成的住宅里做饭

Shen Yeqiu (right), a veteran worker with the Bengbu Glass Works in Anhui Province, cooks a meal in the house he built using his own funds.

住 Housing | 097

1990

广东广州,白天鹅宾馆成为内地首批五星级酒店之一。酒店开业于1983年,是内地首家由中国人设计、建设和经营的五星级酒店,被誉为印证改革开放成功的典范

The White Swan Hotel in Guangzhou, Guangdong Province was one of the first group of five-star hotels established in the mainland. Opened in 1983, the hotel was designed, constructed and operated purely by Chinese. It was praised as a model of successful reform and opening up.

1991 上海，华东第一村——旗忠村的住宅
Residences of Qizhong Village in Shanghai, known as the No.1 Village in East China.

1992 山东莱州，三山岛渔村的新式住房
New residences in the Fishermen's Village on Sanshan Island in Laizhou, Shandong Province.

1993 北京,在菊儿胡同建成的新四合院住宅
A new quadrangle house built in ancient Juer Hutong in Beijing.

1994 天津，建设中的居民住宅。天津市历史上规模最大的市区危陋平房改造工程，从 1994 年初正式启动，到 1999 年底超额完成任务，历时整整六年

New residential buildings in Tianjin. A renovation project to replace dangerous and shabby bungalows in Tianjin, the largest project of its kind in Tianjin, was officially launched in early 1994 and overfulfilled by the end of 1999.

1995 上海，古北新区是二十世纪九十年代"上海十大新景观"中唯一的商品住宅建筑群。位于市中心的传统石库门房子消失了，代之而起的是现代化装修的商业大厦

Gubei New Area was the only commercial residential complex among the 10 new landscapes of Shanghai in the 1990s. Traditional Shikumen houses in the center of the city disappeared, making way for modern decorated commercial buildings.

1996 西藏拉萨,市区新建了一千多万平方米的藏式住宅
More than 10 million square meters of Tibetan-style housing were built in downtown Lhasa, Tibet Autonomous Region.

1997 / 除夕夜，山东潍坊，杨家埠一户村民过年时家中的布置——典型的传统与现代相结合
Family decorations featuring a combination of tradition and modernity adorn a farmer's house in Yangjiabu, Weifang, Shandong Province.

住 Housing | 105

1998 / 在北京住宅与房地产展销会上，参展项目以商品住宅为主。当年，国务院发布《关于进一步深化城镇住房制度改革，加快住房建设的通知》，要求自下半年起全面实行住宅商品化

In the mid-1990s, major exhibits of a residential and real estate fairs in Beijing are commercial housing. In this year, the State Council issued a *Notice on Further Deepening the Reform of Urban Housing System and Speeding up Housing Construction*, calling for the full implementation of housing commercialization from the second half of the year.

1999 北京，京郊共同致富第一村——韩村河村的住宅
Residences in Hancunhe Village, the No.1 Village in Beijing's Suburb, that rode the reform tide to affluence.

住 Housing | 107

2000 浙江温岭，一位教师的家。中国百姓开始注重住宅的内部装修
A teacher's home in Wenling, Zhejiang Province. Chinese people begin to stress interior decoration of housing.

2001 / 北京，大兴区兴涛花园一角。住宅的外部环境开始成为人们选择房子的重要因素
A shot of the Xingtao Garden in Daxing District, Beijing. The consumers pay much attention to the external environment of housing quarters.

住 Housing | 109

2002 / 北京，一些符合政策的住房需求者在挑选经济适用房
The government enacted policies concerning the distribution of affordable housing. Picture shows people looking at such housing in Beijing.

2003 / 江苏南京，银行为购房者办理个人住房贷款。2000年以来，内地一二线大城市的商品房市场日益火爆，各大银行的贷款业务量也随之飞速增长

In the new century, banks in Nanjing, Jiangsu Province, increasingly granted loans to home buyers. Since 2000, the commercial housing market in the mainland's first and second-tier cities became increasingly popular, and the loan business of major banks has also increased rapidly.

住 Housing

2004 / 青海海南藏族自治州，一户牧民的藏式特色住宅
A Tibetan-style residence for a herder's family in the Hainan Tibetan Autonomous Prefecture in Qinghai.

2005 上海，国际家居零售业巨头"宜家家居"在漕溪北路开设的分店。中国建材市场的火爆刺激了国际建材零售公司的在华扩张，越来越多的"洋家具""洋建材"开始进入中国人的日常生活

IKEA, an international home retail giant, opened a store at Caoxi Road North in Shanghai in 2005. The booming building materials market stimulated the expansion of international building materials retail companies in China. More and more "foreign furniture" and "foreign building materials" became available in the country.

2006 黑龙江黑河，嫩江县临江乡铁古砬子村村民从破旧的老房子，搬到了由县里统一规划、统一设计建造的新型住房
New and comparatively modern dwelling houses for residents of Tiegulazi Village, Linjiang Township, Nenjiang County, Hehei, Heilongjiang Province.

2007 / 上海，陆家嘴地区一些高档住宅正在建设中。随着全国房地产市场的火爆，各地都出现了高档商品房
Construction of high-grade residential buildings in full swing in Lujiazui, Shanghai. With booming real estate business, high-grade dwelling houses were in great demand in China.

住 Housing

2008 / 西藏拉萨，首期廉租住宅小区——绿色阳光家园
Green Sunshine Home, the first low-rent residential quarters in Lhasa, Tibet Autonomous Region.

2009 / 北京，一个楼盘卧室样板间。精装修新房受到越来越多购房者的青睐
A typical bedroom in a building in Beijing. Refined decoration of new houses is increasingly demanded by buyers.

2010 / 四川广安，武胜县白坪乡的农家小洋楼
Rural villas in Baiping Town, Wusheng County, Guang'an, Sichuan Province.

2011 / 浙江嘉兴，居民等候公租房电脑选号结果
People waiting for public rental housing computer selection results in Jiaxing, Zhejiang Province.

住 Housing | 119

2012 / 云南红河，河口瑶山三百余户农民告别危房喜迁新居
More than 300 farmers who used to live in dangerous houses in Yaoshan Town, Hekou Yao Ethnic Group Autonomous County, Honghe Hani and Yi Ethnic Autonomous Prefecture in Yunnan, have moved into new houses.

2013 / 北京,一位居民家的花园。随着人们购房心态的理智和成熟,现在大家更看重的是有益身心健康的绿色住宅
A private garden of a Beijing resident, showing how, nowadays, people seek a green housing environment good for physical and mental health.

2014

江苏张家港,"华夏第一钢村"——永联村将农村打造成媲美城镇的宜居之地。永联村走出了一条以工业化带动城镇化建设,进而全面实现农业、农村现代化的发展路径

Yonglian Village, known as the No. 1 Steel Village in China in Zhangjiagang, Jiangsu Province, in recent years was hailed as a livable place comparable to cities and towns. Yonglian Village has embarked on a development path of urbanization driven by industrialization, and then realizing the modernization of agriculture and rural areas in an all-round way.

2015 / 湖北武汉，位于武汉市后官湖风景区的合众人寿养老社区。随着人口老龄化的加剧和普通商品房市场竞争的激烈化，很多企业将目光转向了养老地产。休闲娱乐、医疗保健、生态环保等成为部分养老地产项目的"标配"
Union Life Insurance Pension Community in the Houguan Lake Scenic Area in Wuhan, Hubei Province. With growth of the aging population and the intensification of the competition in the ordinary commercial housing market, many housing enterprises have turned their attention to pension real estate. Leisure entertainment, health care, environmental protection, etc. become part of the pension real estate project.

2016 云南马龙，大凹子村村民已入住新民居。从同年 6 月份开始，全村三十一户苗族群众陆续搬进了新家
Villagers of the Dawazi Village in Malong, Yunnan Province have moved into their new homes. Also, in the middle of the year, 31 Miao people in the village also moved into new homes.

2017 / 浙江武义，大田乡碗铺村刚建成对外营业的随园生态民宿，天天客满

Wanpu Village in Datian Town, Wuyi, Zhejiang Province is involved in tourist reception work nowadays, with special rooms set aside for people who come for ecological touriam. Such rooms are all booked up every day.

住 Housing | 125

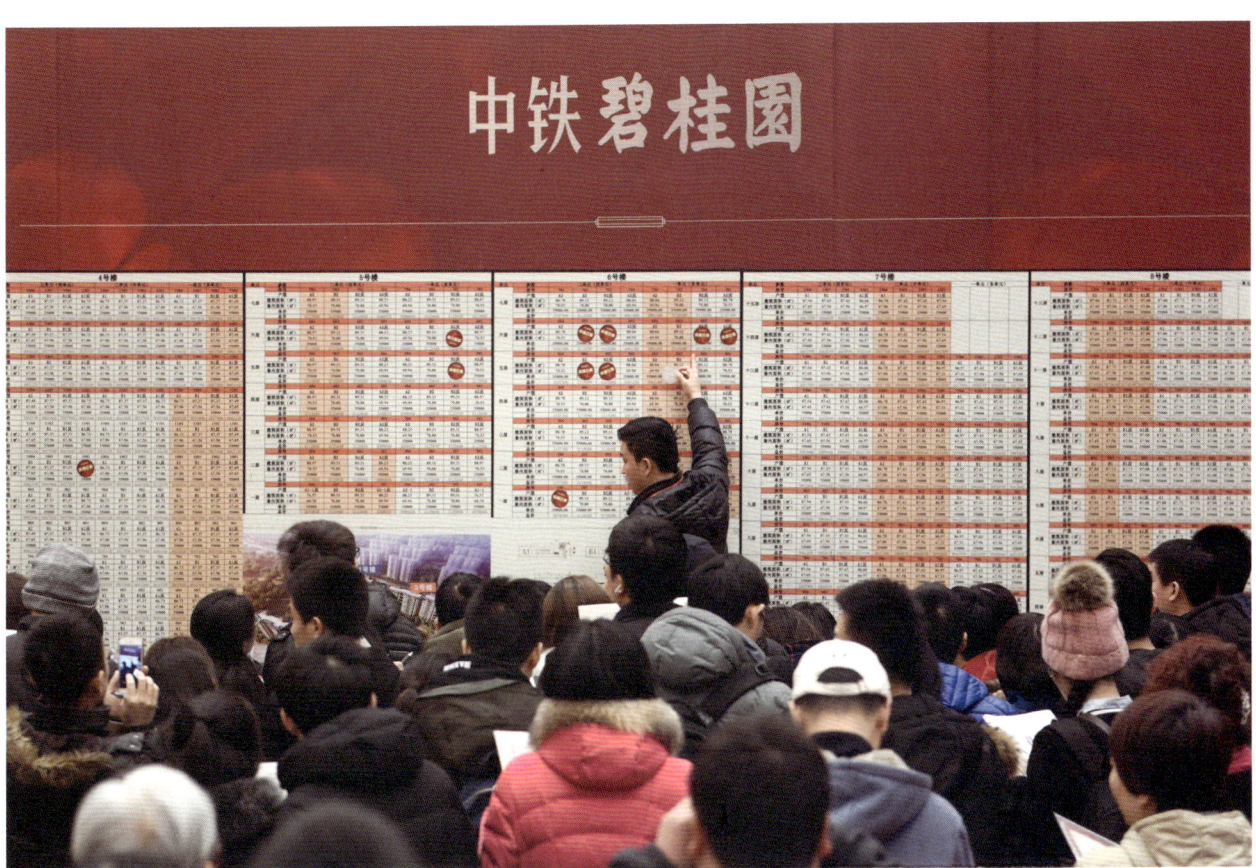

2018 北京，海淀区首个共有产权房开盘选房。这是国家抑制房价增长过快的有力举措

The first shared ownership housing opens for public selection in Haidian District, Beijing. Through construction of this kind of housing, the government seeks to curb inflationary house prices.

行

Chapter IV Travel

第四章

中国人的40年
CHANGES IN CHINESE LIFE IN 40 YEARS

1979 湖南长沙，设在街头的自行车打气站，群众可以随时到这里给自行车打气。自行车是当时中国人最重要的代步工具
Bicycle air-supply station in Changsha, Hunan Province, in 1979. Bicycles were the most important tool for the Chinese at that time, and such stations were a welcome sight for cyclists.

1980 北京故宫,"红旗"牌轿车作为稀罕物只供游人拍照
Red Flag car parks in the Imperial Palace in Beijing as something rare for visitors to take photos.

1981 北京东单，人力三轮车。二十世纪九十年代以前，人力三轮车一直是北京城里的一种普遍而廉价的交通工具。如今，这种老式的脚踏三轮车已经成为了北京胡同游的特色之一

Manpower tricycles in Dongdan, Beijing. Before the 1990s, tricycles were a popular and inexpensive means of transportation in Beijing. Nowadays, such old-fashioned pedal power is used to carry tourists to visit the narrow hutong lanes.

行 Travel | 131

1982 新疆，塔里木盆地的一百万户维吾尔族农民大都购置了畜力胶轮车。图为库车县农民乘着自己的马车去赶集
Some one million Uyghur farmers in the Tarim Basin, Xinjiang, purchased animal-powered rubber-tired vehicles. The picture shows farmers from Kuche County driving their horse-drawn cart to visit local fairs.

1983

广东，梅县侨乡第一次降下民航飞机，吸引了群众围观

For the first time in history a civil aviation aircraft lands at the airport in Meixian County in Guangdong Province, known as the hometown for numerous overseas Chinese, attracting crowds of people.

1984 宁夏,吴忠市东风乡解放村回族农民韩金祥(右)先后购买了两台手扶拖拉机,既种责任田又搞运输

Han Jinxiang (right), a Hui farmer from Jiefang Village, Dongfeng Township, Wuzhong City, Ningxia Hui Autonomous Region, bought two walking tractors in the early 1980's to carry out farming and engage in transportation.

1985 贵州锦屏，拥挤的公共汽车。公共汽车在全国日益普及，但是由于车辆少，乘客多，很多地区的公共汽车异常拥挤
Crowded buses in Jinping, Guizhou Province. Buses were being popularized throughout the country, but in many areas they were unusually crowded because there weren't enough of them to meet the demand.

1986 上海,一对夫妇欢欢喜喜地把刚买的洗衣机用平板三轮车拉回家。在那个时期,平板三轮车是主要的载货交通工具
The couple has purchased a washing machine that they transport back home with the aid of a flat tricycle, the major form of transportation at that time.

1987 中国第一家地方国营航空公司——上海航空公司，空乘人员在上海飞往北京的航班上为乘客服务
A plane of Shanghai Airline, China's first local State-owned civil aviation entity, is seen flying from Shanghai to Beijing.

行 Travel | 137

1988 / 内地首条高速公路——沪嘉高速公路建成通车。到 2017 年 3 月,中国高速公路通车总里程超过美国,位居世界第一
The Shanghai-Jiaxing Expressway, the first such road on the Chinese mainland, completed between 1984 and 1988. The total length of China's expressway network exceeded that of the United States by March 2017 to rank first in the world.

1989 浙江温州，三轮汽车是当地农村重要的交通工具
Tri-trucks were an important means of transportation in rural areas in Wenzhou, Zhejiang Province.

1990 广东，阳春渡口摆渡船
A ferry in Yangchun, Guangdong Province.

1991 　上海，下班高峰时段的自行车大军。到二十世纪八十年代末期，中国自行车保有量达到了五亿辆。靠自行车，中国人第一次整体改变了自己的速度

The cycling army during the rush hour in Shanghai. By the end of the 1980s, the number of bicycles in China reached 500 million, providing more mobility and faster speed for Chinese people.

1992 河北，某村落中的驴车和汽车形成了鲜明对照。在二十世纪九十年代初期，桑塔纳、拉达、达契亚等汽车能够彰显一个人的"高贵"身份

Donkey cart and automobiles in a village in Hebei Province. In the early 1990s, owning a Santana, Lada, Dacia and another brand of car highlighted the dignity of an individual.

1993 北京，长长的"面的"队伍是街头一景。这些黄色"面的"价格便宜、耗油少，主要是天津生产的大发微型面包车
Minibuses throng the streets of Beijing. Most of these yellow vehicles were used as taxis, featuring a cheap price and less fuel consumption. Picture shows Dafa minibuses manufactured in Tianjin.

1994 四川，重庆至万县长江段开通了水翼船，缩短了游客游览三峡的旅途时间
Hydrofoil boats become a travel mode on the Yangtze River from Chongqing to Wanxian in Sichuan Province, shortening the travel time for tourists visiting the Three Gorges.

1995 从武汉开往长沙的列车上，一位男子在拥挤的车厢中，躺在了硬座座椅靠背上。二十世纪九十年代，全国的火车大多数还是"绿皮车"，由于车次较少，火车内常常是异常拥挤

A male passenger on his "hard seat" in a train from Wuhan in Hubei Province to Changsha in Hunan Province. In the 1990s, most of the passenger trains in the country were still designated as "green trains" with hard seats. Because of the small number available, the trains were often very crowded.

1996 京九线建成通车，它是中国一次性建成双线线路最长的一项宏伟铁路工程

The Beijing-Kowloon Railway Line was completed and opens to traffic in the mid-1990's. It is the longest dual-track railway in China.

1997 牡丹江开往长汀的列车上提供放映服务
Mini-film shown to entertain passengers in the Mudanjiang-Changting Railway.

1998 上海开往北京的列车上,乘客在打电话。在手机未普及的年代,乘客只能通过铁路线路与外界联络
A passenger making a phone call on the Shanghai-Beijing Railway. Before the popularization of cell phones, passengers managed to get in touch with people outside the train through such telephones.

1999 海南,琼州海峡轮渡。海南省建省之初,琼州海峡轮渡是人们进出海南岛的主要工具
Ferry in the Qiongzhou Strait in Hainan Province. At that time, people crossed to the southernmost island by such ferries.

2000 / 北京，万头攒动看车展。2000 年左右，私家车开始在全国普及，除了"老三样"捷达、桑塔纳和富康，汽车市场上出现了更多的品牌和车型

Crowded auto show in Beijing. Private cars begin to spread throughout the country in the late 1990s. The automobile market was crowded with more brands and models, such as Jetta, Santana and Fukang.

2001 中国铁路大提速。10月21日,广深铁路再次提速后,初步实现广州与深圳间城际旅客列车的公交化。图为驶入广州东站的国产蓝箭高速列车

China raises train speed. On October 21 2001, the Guangzhou-Shenzhen Railway began to feature faster trainer runs, preliminary realization of inter-city passenger trains shuttling often between Guangzhou and Shenzhen. Here is a Blue Arrow high-speed train entering Guangzhou East Railway Station.

行 Travel | 151

2002

上海，世界上第一条商业化运营的磁悬浮示范线胜利通车

The world's first commercially-operated Maglev Demonstration Line successfully opens to traffic in Shanghai.

2003 / 6月6日,世界第一拱"卢浦大桥"桥头字吊装成功,6月28日全线通车。卢浦大桥是当今世界跨度第二长的钢结构拱桥,也是世界上首座完全采用焊接工艺连接的大型拱桥

The bridgehead of the Lupu Bridge, the first large-scale arch bridge in the world, is successfully hoisted. The bridges opened to traffic in June 28 2003. It is the second longest span steel arch bridge in the world, and it is also the first large-scale arch bridge in the world that completely connected by welding technology.

2004 / 深圳，首列地铁列车到达世界之窗站
The first subway train arrives at the Window on the World Station in Shenzhen.

2005 即将下岗的蒸汽机车和即将上岗的内燃机车仅一墙之隔。近年来,由于高铁快速发展,中国进入"高铁时代"。与此同时,另一个工业革命的产物——蒸汽机车逐渐退出历史舞台

Steam locomotives give way to diesels, separated by a wall. China was able to enter the "high-speed rail era" when steam locomotives, product of the industrial revolution, gradually withdrew from the stage of history.

行 Travel | 155

2006 青海，世界上海拔最高的铁路——青藏铁路全线贯通
Qinghai boasts the world's highest railways. Here, the Qinghai-Tibet Railway is seen in full operation in the first decade of the 21st Century.

2007 东海大桥工程,这是我国第一座真正意义上的跨海大桥
The Donghai Bridge project was China's first sea-crossing bridge in a true sense.

2008 我国第一条城际高速铁路——京津城际高铁正式开通运营
The Beijing-Tianjin Intercity High-Speed Rail, first of its kind in China, went into service.

2009 / 世界上一次性建设里程最长、运营速度最快的铁路——武广高铁客运新干线正式开通运营
The Wuhan-Guangzhou High-speed Railway goes into full operation. It became the passenger train with the longest mileage and the fastest running speed in the world.

2010 2月19日，广西南宁市迎来自驾游返程高峰。在琅东高速路出口收费站，数百辆轿车排成长龙。自驾成为节假日人们出游的首选

Hundreds of cars queue up at a tollgate on the Langdong Expressway in Nanning, Guangxi Zhuang Autonomous Region Region on February 19. During holidays, many people in the city had developed the habit of self-drive tours.

2011 新疆第一条山区高速公路——赛里木湖至果子沟口高速公路
The Sayram Lake-Tarchi Daban Expressway became the first mountainous expressway in the Xinjiang Uygur Autonomous Region.

2012 四川稻城,世界上海拔最高的民航机场启用
The world's highest civil aviation airport, operating in Daocheng in Sichuan Province.

2013 / 西藏，墨脱公路正式通车。这意味着中国最后一个不通公路的县城通车

The opening of the Medog Highway in 2013 put an end to the history of being the last county in China with no highway access.

2014 新疆，一列动车从兰新高铁哈密淀泉特大桥上驶过。兰新高铁是世界上第一条高原高铁
A bullet train crosses Dianquan Bridge on the Lanzhou-Urumqi High-speed Railway in the Xinjiang Uygur Autonomous Region. It became the first high-speed railway on a high plateau in the world.

2015 建设中的港珠澳大桥。全程五十五公里的港珠澳大桥,是世界上最长的跨海大桥,也是中国交通史上技术最复杂、建设要求及标准最高的工程之一,被英国《卫报》誉为"新世界七大奇迹之一"

Construction of the Hong Kong-Zhuhai-Macao Bridge in full swing in 2015. Spanning 55 km, it the longest sea-crossing bridge in the world, whose construction was technically complex and very demanding, calling for the highest standard.

2016 / 杭瑞高速北盘江大桥建成通车。从桥面到谷底的垂直高度为五百六十五米,相当于二百层楼高,该桥是世界上最高的跨江大桥

The Beipan River Bridge on the Hangzhou-Ruili Expressway is completed. It is 560 meters high, equivalent to a 200-storey building, becoming the tallest cross-river bridge in the world.

2017 北京，共享单车成为城市的一道风景。2016年以来，共享单车突然火爆起来，各大城市路边排满了各种颜色的共享单车。这种"创新出行"方式大大方便了市民

Shared bicycles become part of the Beijing landscape. Since 2016, shared bicycles with different colors appeared in huge numbers on the city's streets, greatly satisfying the need of people for convenient urban transportation.

2018 / 贵州贵阳，未来方舟电动汽车充电站正式投入运行。中国近年来大力发展清洁能源汽车，建立起了具有自主知识产权的电动汽车全产业链技术体系

The Future Ark Electric Vehicle Charging Station in Guiyang, Guizhou Province goes into service. With the great efforts China has made to develop clean energy vehicles, it has been able to establish a technical system of an electric vehicle industry chain with independent intellectual property rights.

用

Chapter V Articles for Daily Use

第五章

中国人的40年
CHANGES IN CHINESE LIFE IN 40 YEARS

1979 四川邛崃,前进公社社员在选购自行车。二十世纪七十年代,自行车、缝纫机、手表被称为"三大件"
Commune members in Qionglai, Sichuan Province, shop for bicycles. In the 1970s, bicycles, sewing machines and wrist watches were called the "three basic needs for a household".

1980 吉林洮安，岭下公社红石岭大队的赵淑珍家，添置了缝纫机等生活用品
Zhao Shuzhen, member of the Hongshiling Production Brigade, Lingxia People's Commune has purchased a sewing machine and other daily necessities.

1981　北京西单商场，抢购电视机。二十世纪八十年代，电视机、冰箱和洗衣机被称为新"三大件"
Consumers shop for TV sets at the Beijing Xidan Shopping Center. In the 1980s, TV sets, refrigerators and washing machines became the new "three basic needs for a household".

1982 一位摄影师为孩子拍照。照相机对普通百姓来说还是个稀罕物
Taking a picture of children. Cameras were rare for ordinary people for a long time.

1983 / 吉林怀德，玻璃城子乡参加技术培训班的农民们带着录音机在课堂上录制农业技术课程
Farmers attending a technical training course in Bolichengzi Township, Huaide, Jilin Province. They record the lectures on agrotechnology for after-class review and application.

用 Articles for Daily Use | 175

1984

河南沁阳，西向乡五街村的居民竞相购买高档家用电器。图为一户农民家中新添置的洗衣机

Thanks to the reforms, residents of Wujie Village, Xixiangyang Town, Henan Province, were able to equip their homes with high-end household electrical appliances. The picture shows a new washing machine in a farmer's home.

1985 北京大兴，留民营村家家都装起了沼气灶。当地居民基本上用沼气烧水煮饭，既方便又卫生

Modernization reaches Liuminying Villages of Daxing in Beijing, in the shape of biogas stoves to boil water and cook, a method both convenient and hygienic and good for the environment.

用 Articles for Daily Use | 177

1986 甘肃甘南藏族自治州，玛曲县尼玛乡藏族牧民选购生活用品时，以地摊形式为主

Herdsmen of the Tibetan ethnic group living in Nyma Town, Maqu County, Gannan Tibetan Autonomous Prefecture in Gansu Province, purchase articles for daily use mainly from street stalls.

1987

北京，春节庙会上孩子们争相购买风车。八零后这一代人的童年都会有这样的风车陪伴

Children purchasing toy windmills at a Spring Festival temple fair in Beijing. Many people born in the 1980s grew up with toy windmills as part of their young lives.

用 Articles for Daily Use | 179

1988 / 河南洛阳，人们争相抢购冰箱
People purchasing refrigerators in Luoyang, Henan Province.

1989 上海，第一百货商店保温瓶柜台前挤满了抢购新式保温瓶的人
Consumers purchasing vacuum thermos flasks in new styles at the No.1 Department Store in Shanghai.

用 Articles for Daily Use | 181

1990 / 江苏，一位店员向顾客推荐录像带。观看录像带是二十世纪八九十年代人们娱乐的主要方式

A shop assistant recommends video tapes to customers in Jiangsu Province. Watching videos became the main mode of entertainment in the 1980s and 1990s.

1991 湖北巴东，三峡山区，沙发等家具是结婚时主要的嫁妆
Sofas and other furniture formed an essential part of a marriage dowry for girls wedding in the Three Gorges mountainous area in Badong, Hubei Province.

用 Articles for Daily Use | 183

1992 / 广东宝安，沙井镇万丰村投资三百万元，为全村五百五十户农民装上了国内外程控直拨电话，成为内地第一个程控电话村

Wanfeng Village in Baoan, Guangdong Province invested a total of three million Yuan to install domestic program-controlled telephones for all households in the village, amounting to 550 sets.

1993 北京，BP机成为人们日常通信的常用工具。在当时流行一句话："有事您呼我。"别一部BP机在腰上，一阵滴滴答答的传呼声响起，会引来许多羡慕的目光

The beeper was, for a while, a common tool for daily communication in Beijing. One often heard people saying: "Call me if there is something." A person displaying a beeper on their waist belt was a source of general envy.

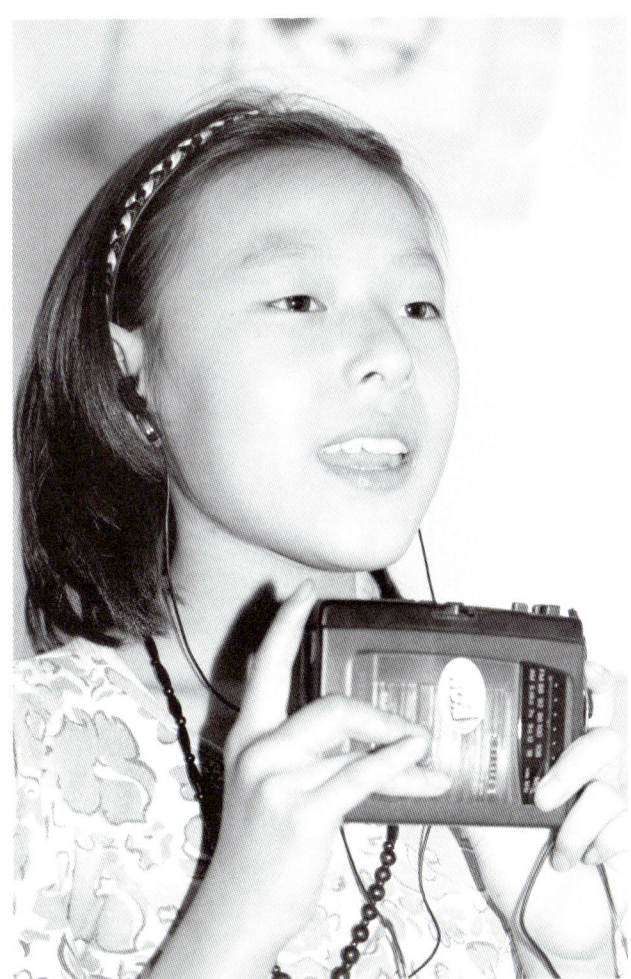

1994 磁带随身听成为了青少年学习和娱乐的必备用品。那时候很多青少年让家里买随身听的理由是要练习英语听力，但是最后更多的是用来听流行歌曲

A walkman cassette tape machine became an essential necessity for youngsters for learning and entertainment. The main "excuse" at the start was that it was needed for learning English, but, eventually, people began using them to listen to pop music.

1995 海南海口,用于婚礼的婚车。二十世纪九十年代,婚礼开始流行车队接亲
Caravan of wedding cars in Haikou, Hainan Province. This became a popular scene for marriages in the 1990s.

用 Articles for Daily Use

1996 北京，中关村一家电脑产品门店。个人电脑及各种电子词典开始兴起

A shot of a computer store at Zhongguancun district in Beijing. Personal computers and various electronic dictionaries became very popular from the 1990s.

1997 北京，高温使市民对空调的需求大大增加。图为北京古桥电器公司积极筹备货源满足顾客需求

Air-conditioners increasingly were in great demand to deal with the oppressive heat of summer. Picture shows the Guqiao Electrical Appliance Company well stocked with air-conditioners.

1998

辽宁沈阳,随着学校中电脑知识的普及教育和个人计算机的全面进入家庭,越来越多的青少年开始通过互联网学习知识、同朋友沟通、交换信息

With the popularization of computer knowledge in schools in Shenyang, Liaoning Province, and the full entry of personal computers into ordinary families, more and more teenagers began to learn how to browse Internet for knowledge, contact with friends and exchange of information.

1999 新疆塔什库尔干，塔吉克族牧民艾拉提一家在看电视。1978 年前，县城没有一座像样的建筑，只有一排排外形单一、简陋矮小的土木小屋。二十多年过去，在各级政府的帮助和高原人的艰苦努力下，塔吉克人的生活发生了巨大变化
Erati, herder of the Tajik ethnic group in the Xinjiang Uygur Autonomous Region, is watching TV at home. Before China introduced the reform and opening-up program in late 1978, there was no real evidence of architecture in the county town of Tashkurgan, only virtually featureless low-lying adobe houses. In a short span of some 20 years, however, the county town witnessed great changes and people there now lead a better life.

用 Articles for Daily Use

2000 上海，诺基亚专卖店员工在仔细为购买手机的顾客介绍产品性能。2000 年前后，诺基亚、摩托罗拉、爱立信等国外手机品牌进入中国市场，标志着手机开始普及

Staff of a Nokia store explaining the performance of cell phones to a potential purchaser in Shanghai. Around the year 2000, Nokia, Motorola, Ericsson and other foreign mobile phone brands entered the Chinese market in force, generating explosive growth in mobile phone use.

2001 / "中国国际摄影器材与数码影像科技博览会"在北京国际展览中心开幕。这是观众在展台前试用小型数码相机和家用摄像机。从 2001 年开始,数码小家电在中国市场热销

The China International Photographic Equipment and Digital Imaging Technology Exposition opens at the Beijing International Exhibition Center. Picture shows visitors trying out a small digital cameras and home camcorders at a booth. Since 2001, digital home appliances have been selling well in the Chinese market.

2002 北京，某电器公司的工作人员在中国国际家用电器展览会上介绍一款具有抽油烟机功能的微波炉。让繁琐的家务变得轻松而富有乐趣的家电受到越来越多百姓的青睐。智能化、人性化、多功能已成为家电业发展的趋势

Staff with an electrical appliance company introduce a microwave oven with the function of a lampblack machine at the China International Household Appliances Exhibition in Beijing. Increasing numbers of people sought furniture and appliances to remove the tedium from housework and make it fun. Intelligence, humanization and multi-function became the trend of the household appliance industry.

中国人的 40 年 CHANGES IN CHINESE LIFE IN 40 YEARS

2003 / 两位年轻人正在某品牌数码产品的体验中心试用笔记本电脑。为让消费者亲自感受产品性能，众多国际知名品牌，如索尼、IBM、惠普、三星等，相继在各大城市设立体验中心，打出了"体验消费"的招牌

Two young people try out notebook computers in the experience center of a branded digital product. In order to let consumers feel the performance of the product as part of the sales promotion program, many famous international brands such as Sony, IBM, HP and Samsung set up such experience centers in major cities.

2004 被称为"绿色手机"的小灵通,以其辐射小和话费低廉的优点,深受消费者喜爱
Personal Handy Phone System (PHS), the "green mobile phone", is much loved by consumers for its advantages of small radiation and low telephone charges.

2005　贵州贵阳，公交车上安装了数字移动电视
A digital mobile TV installed on a bus in Guiyang, Guizhou Province.

用 Articles for Daily Use | 197

2006

上海，一名小学生拖着拉杆书包上学。拉杆书包受到了各地小学生的青睐
A pupil drags along a school bag in Shanghai. This kind of schoolbag became very popular with pupils everywhere.

2007 / 北京，环卫工人骑上了新型环保电动车
Sanitation workers in Beijing ride on new environmentally-friendly electric vehicles.

用 Articles for Daily Use | 199

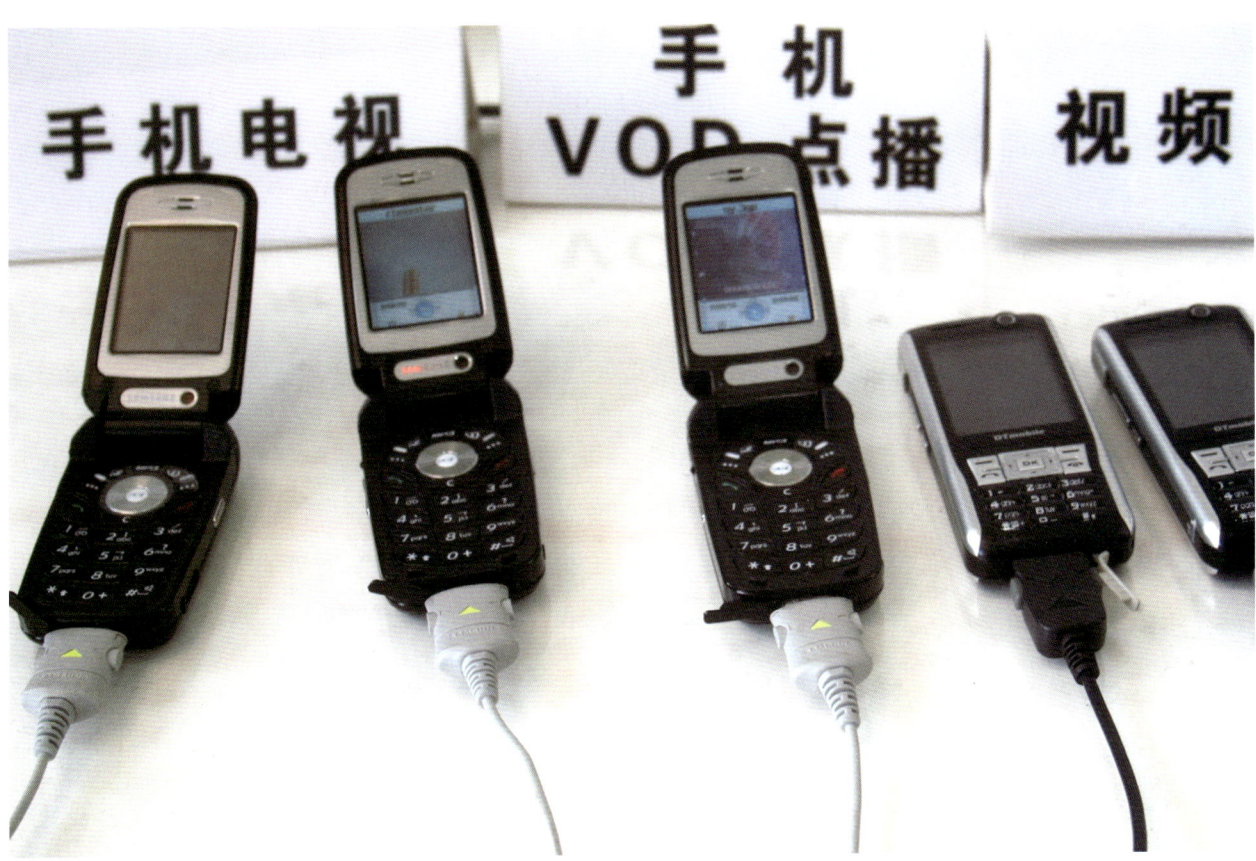

2008 / 随着 3G 通信技术的发展，手机电视等通信工具受到了年轻人的青睐
With the development of 3G communications technology, young Chinese began to favor communication tools such as mobile TV.

2009 / 湖北宜昌，市民在苏宁电器专卖店选购 TCL 电视。液晶电视在电器市场上崭露头角，受到广大消费者的喜爱
Purchasing a TCL TV in the Suning Appliance Store in Yichang, Hubei Province. Liquid crystal TV (LCTV) began to enjoy good sales in the Chinese market.

用 Articles for Daily Use | 201

2010

北京，顾客在三里屯苹果专卖店试用平板电脑。当日8时，苹果无线网络版平板电脑在内地市场正式开始销售

Customers trying tablet computers at the Apple Store in Sanlitun, Beijing. At 8 o'clock on that day, Apple Wireless Internet Tablet PC officially went on sale in the mainland market.

2011 北京，一位小朋友在北京图书订货会上体验彩色儿童电子书，这是该书展首次设立数字出版专区。各种用于数字阅读的电子设备相继面市

A boy experiences color children's e-books at a book fair in Beijing. This is the first time that a digital publishing sector was established in a book fair. Various e-book devices have been invented for digital reading.

用 Articles for Daily Use | 203

2012   中国启用电子护照。中国电子护照与普通护照相比，增加了存储申请人指纹及签名等数字化个人资料的智能芯片，采用数字签名技术对存储的个人资料加以保护，提高了护照防伪和安全性能

China introduces electronic passports. Compared with the ordinary one, the electronic passport contained a smart chip to store digital personal data such as the applicant's fingerprint and signature, and used digital signature technology to protect the stored personal data. It improves the security and security performance of passports.

2013 北京，智能分类垃圾桶。2010年起，北京开始在全市逐步推行垃圾分类。实际上，这种"智能分类"垃圾桶在杭州等多个城市都有试点。这些垃圾桶无一例外都用上了"二维码"扫描这一时下流行的互动方式，并对做得好的住户予以奖励

Intelligent sorting bins in Beijing. Since 2010, Beijing has gradually adopted garbage classification in the whole city. In fact, the "intelligent classification" trash has been in pilot use in many cities, such as Hangzhou in Zhejiang Province. All of these trash cans use a popular interactive method of "two-dimensional code" scanning and reward households for being conscientious.

2014 / 四川凉山彝族自治州,在大山深处,户用光伏系统解决了当地居民的用电问题
A household photovoltaic system adopted to solve the electricity supply problem plaguing local residents in the deep mountains in Liangshan Yi Ethnic Autonomous Prefecture of Sichuan Province.

2015 北京，纪念中国人民抗日战争暨世界反法西斯战争胜利七十周年大阅兵进行最后一次实景演练，看台上数万观众举起了手机

Tens of thousands of spectators raise their mobile phones during the last live drill in Beijing, held to mark the 70th Anniversary of the Chinese People's War of Resistance Against Japan and the victory of the World Anti-Fascist War.

2016

上海，华山路上的一家菜市场内，消费者结算时选择手机支付的方式
A grocery market on Huashan Road, Shanghai, where many consumers pay for their purchases using mobile payment technology.

2017

上海,中国家电及消费电子博览会,参观者在展会上观看一款家庭服务机器人。智能家居已经悄然进入普通百姓家庭

At the China Home Appliances and Consumer Electronics Fair in Shanghai, the audiences watch the performance of a smart home service robot, which has quietly entered ordinary families.

2018 / 北京，在海淀区德政路自动送货的京东配送机器人
A Jingdong parcels distribution robot operating on Dezheng Road in the Haidian District of Beijing.

教育

Chapter VI Education

第六章

中国人的 40 年
CHANGES IN CHINESE LIFE IN 40 YEARS

1979 参加完当年全国高考的学生们。1978 年，我国恢复了高考制度

Students celebrate finishing the national college entrance examination. In 1978, China resumed the examination after years of suspension during the "cultural revolution" (1966-1976).

1980 / 江西南昌，教师王武编写的小学室内体育游戏教材深受欢迎

Textbook on primary school indoor sports games, compiled by Teacher Wang Wu, is very much enjoyed by pupils in Nanchang, Jiangxi Province.

1981 中国科协、国家民委、教育部、共青团中央和全国妇联在北京共同举办了"全国少数民族青少年科技夏令营"

The National Summer Camp for Minority Youth Science and Technology in Beijing. It is jointly organized by the Chinese Association for Science and Technology, the State Ethnic Affairs Commission, Ministry of Education, the Central Committee of the Communist Youth League and the All-China Women's Federation.

1982

河北安新，县城小学的学生。教育一直是党和国家最重视的问题，1982年党的"十二大"第一次把教育列为经济发展的战略重点之一

Students of Anxin County Primary School in Hebei Province. In 1982, the 12th National Congress of the Communist Party of China made education one of the strategic priorities of economic development for the first time, a move emphasizing the high importance to education.

1983 / 北京，中国人民大学科学社会主义系学生在宿舍谈读书体会
Students of the Department of Scientific Socialism of Renmin University of China in Beijing discuss their reading experience in the dormitory.

1984 陕西，西安企业子弟小学的孩子们庆祝儿童节

Students of the Primary School for Children of Factory Workers in Xi'an, Shaanxi Province, mark the June 1 Children's Day.

1985 吉林农安，中国首个教师节前夕，县委、县政府给全县三十四家三代以上从事教育工作的教师颁发"教育世家"光荣匾

On the eve of China's first Teacher's Day in 1985, the CPC Nong'an County Committee of Jilin Province and the Nong'an county government issued commemorative plaques to 34 families engaged in school education for more than three generations.

1986

北京，劲松一小的学生们在做课间哑铃操。1986年7月1日，《中华人民共和国义务教育法》施行，适龄儿童、少年接受义务教育的权利得到保障

Students of Jinsong No.1 Primary School in Beijing perform dumbbell exercises during the morning break. On July 1, 1986, the *Law of the People's Republic of China on Compulsory Education* came into force, guaranteeing the right of school-age children to receive compulsory education.

1987 上海,卢湾中学的同学们在新建成的体育馆里上体育课
Students of Luwan Middle School in Shanghai attend a PE class in the newly-built school gymnasium.

教育 Education | 221

1988 / 湖北襄阳，农村女青年陶桂芬应邀当上了农业中学教师，教授学生食用菌生产技术
Tao Guifen, a young rural woman in Xiangyang, Hubei Province, employed as a teacher in an agricultural middle school. She teaches production techniques of edible fungi.

1989 / 山西太原，桃园小学的老师正在指导学生阅读课外书籍
Teachers of Taoyuan Primary School in Taiyuan, Shanxi Province instruct students on how to read extracurricular books.

1990 / 北京，中央广播电视大学利用电视教学
TV education programs are launched in Beijing by the Central Radio and Television University.

1991

安徽金寨,桃岭乡三合中心小学的学生苏明娟正在认真地听讲。"大眼睛"苏明娟这张照片发表后,被国内各大媒体转载,"大眼睛"成为了"希望工程"的标志

Su Mingjuan, a student of Sanhe Central Primary School of Taoling Township, Jinzhai, Anhui Province, "listening carefully". This picture was published by the media, and Su, nicknamed "Big Eyes", became a symbol of the Hope Project, promoting education in remote rural areas.

1992 / 浙江江山，江郎山地区一所学校的孩子们，在老师的带领下参加"一日游"活动
Students of a primary school in Jianglangshan area, Jiangshan, Zhejiang Province, enjoy a one-day tour organized by their teachers.

1993 福建永春，美岭村为儿童创造免费上学的条件

Meiling Village in Yongchun, Fujian Province, symbolized how small communities created conditions for children to go to school free of charge.

1994 上海，民工学校首批学员正式结业并举行结业典礼。这是我国首个以培养农民工综合素质为目的的公益学校
Graduation ceremony for the first batch of trainees of the School for Migrant Workers in Shanghai. The school was the first public welfare school in China to improve the quality of migrant worker education.

1995 新疆，天山草原上的尼勒克县乌拉斯台乡草原小学，吸收了一百多名哈萨克族牧民的孩子上学
The Grassland Primary School of Wulastai Township in Nilke County, Tianshan Grassland, Xinjiang Uygur Autonomous Region, recruited more than 100 Kazakh herdsmen's children for formal education.

1996 / 江苏南京，全国第一位受"希望工程"资助考上研究生的农家子弟张宗友，来到南京大学研究生院报到入学
Zhang Zongyou, admitted to the Graduate School of Nanjing University in Jiangsu Province, was the first student to complete his college studies with funding provided by the Hope Project.

1997

福建安溪,清溪城隍祖庙经改造后变为小学
City God Ancestral Temple in Qingxi of Anxi, in Fujian Province, transformed into a primary school.

教育 Education | 231

1998 / 北京，随着"出国留学热"的出现，国际教育也瞄准了中国市场，在中国国际贸易中心举办的英国教育展掀起了热潮
With many people in China sending their children to study abroad, international education authorities began to develop a strong interest in the China market. A British education exhibition showing the state of education in the U.K., held in the International Trade Center in China, helped set off a boom in international study.

1999 广东工业大学应届毕业的大学生身着学士服在校园留影。1999年教育部出台《面向21世纪教育振兴行动计划》，扩大高校招生规模

Graduates from the Guangdong University of Technology in Guangzhou, Guangdong Province. In 1999, the Ministry of Education issued the Action Plan for Education Revitalization in the 21st Century, expanding the enrollment scale of colleges and universities.

2000 湖南,省教委出台全省中小学生"减负"措施,"书包变轻"的孩子们高高兴兴地放学回家

The Provincial Education Commission of Hunan Province issued regulations stipulating measures designed to reduce the burden of primary and secondary school students in the province. Students with lighter schoolbags happily on their way home.

2001 江苏南京，七十二岁老人汪侠如愿以偿地拿到了高考的准考证。这一年，教育部出台新政策，允许二十五周岁以上公民参加高考，彻底放开高校招生的年龄限制

72-year-old man, Wang Xia, is happy to get the admission ticket for the national college entrance examination. In 2001 the Ministry of Education launched a new policy allowing citizens at or over 25 years of age to participate in the national college entrance examination.

教育 Education | 235

2002 / 贵州，贵阳市实验小学师生打破传统教学方式，进行互动式的启蒙英语教育。从 2001 年开始，新一轮国家级基础教育改革实验在全国范围内展开，贵阳是全国最大的几个实验区之一

Teachers and pupils of Guiyang Experimental Primary School break the traditional education mode methods of teaching mainly by teachers to carry out interactive enlightenment English education. In 2001, China launched a new round of national-level basic educational reform experiments nationwide, and Guiyang became one of the largest experimental areas.

2003 河南郑州，一所老年大学的计算机课堂。老年大学是适应社会老龄化、建设终身学习的学习型社会以及和谐社会的需要而发展起来的时代产物，是"终身学习"最恰当的体现

A computer classroom of a senior's university in Zhengzhou, Henan Province. Universities of this kind were set up for the aged to meet the needs for lifelong education and develop a harmonious society.

2004 / 安徽阜阳，四九小学请来当年曾参加抗日战争的越德成老人为学生上国防教育课
The April 9 Primary School in Fuyang, Anhui Province, invited Yue Decheng, who participated in the War of Resistance Against Japan, to lecture on how local people rose to fight the Japanese invaders.

2005 江苏南京，一场别开生面的"开笔破蒙仪式"在夫子庙大成殿举行。近几十年来中国经济的发展，激发了中国人学习传统文化的热情

A ritual is held at Dacheng Hall of the Confucius Temple in Nanjing, Jiangsu Province for people to learn traditional culture. The development of China's economy in the preceding decades fired the enthusiasm of the Chinese for the traditional culture.

2006 山东，高密第二实验小学的"攀登英语"课堂上，小学生们聚精会神地听课。2006年新《义务教育法》的出台推动"两免一补"政策在全国落实，昭示了国家的一种态度：让每一个孩子都有平等接受教育的机会

Pupils attending the "Climbing English" class of the No. 2 Experimental Primary School in Gaomi, Shandong Province. In 2006 the Chinese government promulgated the Compulsory Education Law, containing the policy of "two exemptions (covering tuition and books fees) and one subsidy (gradually subsidizing boarding students' living expenses)", a policy introduced especially for students in poverty-stricken areas in central and western Chinese regions, thus enabling every child to have equal access to education.

2007 / 海南，定南学生观看学校循环生态经济示意图。当地从 2007 年年中开始创建循环生态经济学校
Students in Dingnan, Hainan Province, visit the "circular ecological economy map" of the school. Since the middle of 2007, recycling ecological economy schools have been operating in Dingnan.

2008 四川,汶川地震灾区的孩子们在军营帐篷希望学校内上课
Children in earthquake-stricken areas of Wenchuan, in Sichuan Province, continue their schooling in a military camp.

2009 / 广西昭平，逸夫小学的孩子们高兴地领到了免费教科书。短短几年，我国教育免费的惠民政策，由点及面，覆盖人群越来越多，覆盖范围越来越广

Children at Yifu Primary School in Zhaoping, Guangxi Zhuang Autonomous Region, happily receive free textbooks. Over a period of several years, China's free education policy grew to cover more and more people in poverty-stricken regions.

2010

辽宁辽阳，第十二中学的学生观看自己组装并设计程序的机器人完成任务。2010年，中共中央、国务院印发《国家中长期教育改革和发展规划纲要（2010—2020年）》，提出到2020年基本实现教育现代化，基本形成学习型社会

Students of the No. 12 Middle School in Liaoyang, Liaoning Province, watch a performance of robots they themselves designed and assembled. In 2010, the CPC Central Committee and the State Council issued the Outline of the National Medium and Long-term Educational Reform and Development Plan (2010-2020), proposing that, by 2020, education would be basically modernized and a learning society basically formed.

2011 安徽六安,毛坦厂镇数万群众、师生及学生家长像过节一样欢送考生赴六安赶考。当地学校被称为"超级中学""亚洲最大高考工厂"

Tens of thousands of people, teachers, students and parents of students in Maotanchang Town, Anhui Province, watch high school graduates getting ready to take part in national college entrance examinations in liu'an. Due to the activities of local high schools, known as "super middle schools", the area became known as "the largest university entrance examination factory in Asia".

教育 Education | 245

2012

辽宁沈阳,市儿童活动中心举办的"武舞更精彩"主题活动,丰富了孩子们的课余生活
The City Children's Activity Center in Shenyang, Liaoning Province organizes martial arts and dancing and other activities helping enrich children's extracurricular life.

2013 / 北京大学开设的创业基础课上,学生们在认真聆听
Students of Peking University carefully listen to a basic entrepreneurship course.

2014

北京，来自香港的三位女生在中国人民大学明德楼前合影。2012年，"内地部分高等院校免试招收香港学生"计划开始实施

Three Hong Kong girls pose for a photo in front of the Mingde Building in Renmin University of China. In 2012, some of the institutions of higher learning began to recruit Hong Kong students without a compulsory entrance examination.

2015 | 宁夏,银川外国语实验学校学生在表演国学经典段落,国学教育走进校园
Students of Yinchuan Foreign Languages Experimental School in Ningxia Hui Autonomous Region perform passages from Chinese literary classics. Chinese classics education was a new feature of campus life.

2016 / 北京东城区，体育馆路小学的学生们戴上虚拟现实眼镜，上了一堂特殊的天文课
Pupils of Tiyuguan Road Primary School in Dongcheng District, Beijing wear virtual reality glasses to start a special astronomy class.

2017 山西太原，小学生训练独轮车骑行，培养团队合作精神

Primary school students in Taiyuan City, Shanxi Province training to ride wheelbarrows as part of the teamwork training program.

2018 / 安徽铜陵,义安区钟鸣中心小学科普室里,老师在为参加科学调查体验活动的学生传授编程机器人知识
At the Science Popularization Room of Zhongming Central Primary School in Tongling, Anhui Province, the teacher is teaching a program related to robot knowledge.

科技

Chapter VII Science and Technology

第七章

中国人的40年
CHANGES IN CHINESE LIFE IN 40 YEARS

1979　建设中的葛洲坝水利枢纽工程。它是长江上第一座大型水电站，于 1971 年 5 月开工兴建，1988 年 12 月全部竣工
Gezhouba Dam Water Conservancy Project, the first large hydropower station on the Yangtze River, whose construction began in May 1971 and ended in December 1988.

1980 / 6月，中美两国海洋科学工作者在我国长江口外及其附近的大陆架海区，进行有关海洋沉积作用过程的联合调查

In June, Chinese and American marine scientists conduct a joint survey of marine sedimentation processes in the continental shelf sea areas adjacent to the Yangtze River Estuary.

1981 我国自行设计建造的第一座大型高通量原子反应堆建成,并成功地进行了高功率运行
The first large high-throughput atomic reactor designed and built by China is operating successfully at full power.

1982 / 我国电火箭首次空间飞行试验成功,标志着我国电火箭的研制工作已经进入了一个新阶段,使我国继美、苏、日后,有了一种新型空间微推力火箭发动机

The success of the first space flight test of an electric rocket in China indicates development has entered a new stage, and that the country has joined the U.S., the former Soviet Union and Japan that had achieved breakthroughs in a new type of space micro-thrust rocket engine.

1983

我国科学家首创一套独特的橡胶树栽培技术，并获得了国家发明一等奖

Chinese scientists create a unique set of rubber tree cultivation techniques, winning the first prize of national invention.

1984 / 4月,我国成功地发射了一颗与地球同步定点的卫星,标志着我国航天技术有了新的飞跃

In April, China successfully launched an Earth-synchronized satellite, marking a major step forward in its space technology.

1985 2月，中国南极长城站举行隆重的落成典礼，这是中国在南极建立的第一个科学考察站，标志着我国南极考察进入一个新阶段

In February, the Great Wall Station in Antarctica was inaugurated with a grand ceremony. China's first scientific research station established in the southern polar region marks a new stage in China's work there.

科技 Science and Technology

1986

一位技术人员在操作激光汉字编辑排版系统。中国首个"计算机—激光汉字编辑排版系统"的研制成功是中国印刷技术发展史上的一次重大技术革命，标志着中国发明的、沿袭千年的活字排版进入被现代先进技术代替的新时期

A technician works on a laser Chinese character editing and typesetting system. Success in developing such a system marks a major technological revolution in the history of Chinese printing technology. It means a new era in which movable type typesetting invented by China and followed for a millennium has made way for modern advanced technology.

1987 1月，长春第一汽车制造厂新建和改建的一百五十条具有当代技术水平的生产线同时开动，新型解放牌汽车正式投产
A total of 150 new and reconstructed production lines armed with state-of-the-art technology of the Changchun No. 1 Automobile Manufacturing Plant were put into use in January, along with production of a new type of Jiefang brand automobile.

1988

10月，两束正负电子在一个巨型机器里成功对撞，揭开了我国高能物理研究的新篇章

In October, two positron beams were successful brought into collision in a giant machine, opening a new chapter in the study of high-energy physics in China.

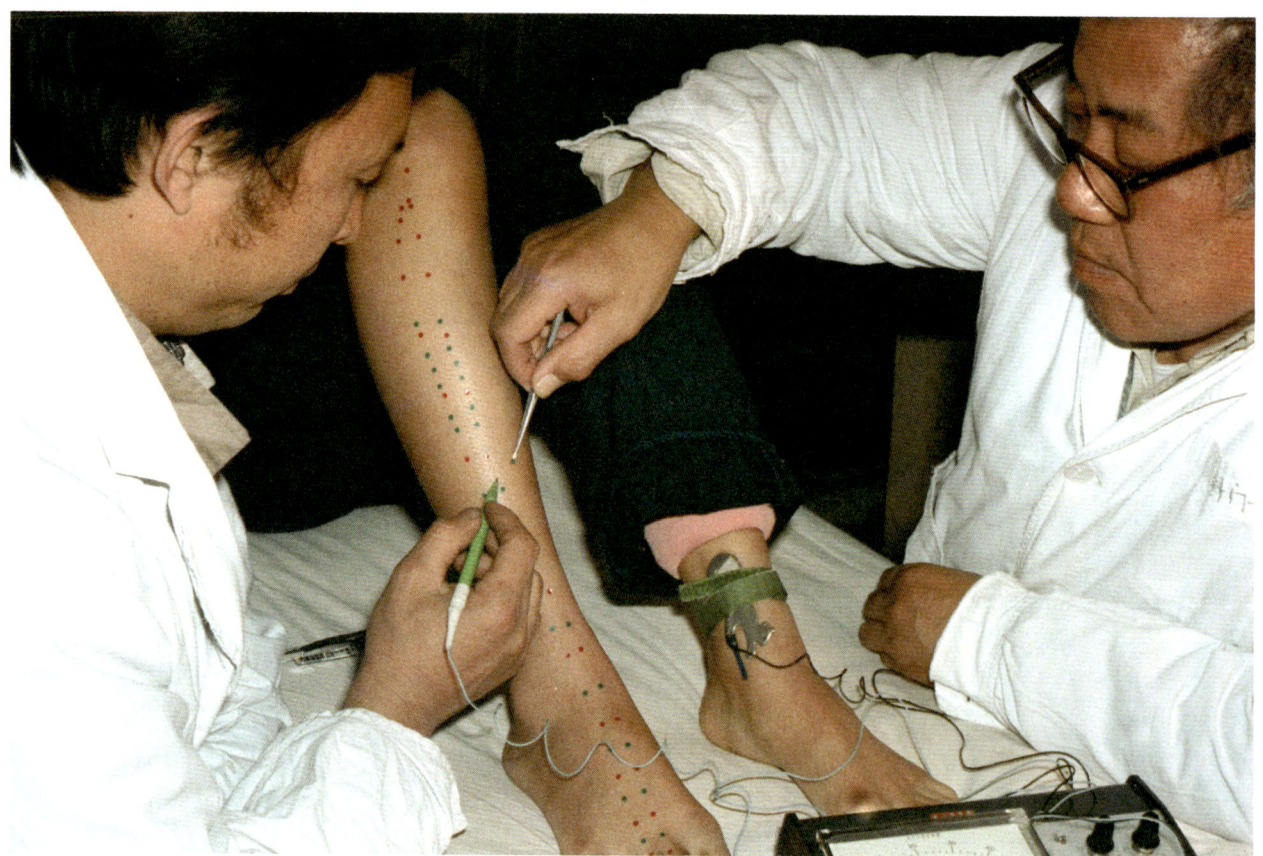

1989 12月，中国科学院生物物理所祝总骧教授运用科学方法测试证明，人及其他动物、植物体内确实普遍存在着经络系统。这一发现后来被运用于中国传统的针灸治疗中，由于定穴准确，对治疗肺气肿、肺心病、帕金森综合征等多种疾病取得很好的疗效

In December, Professor Zhu Zongxiang of the Institute of Biophysics of the Chinese Academy of Sciences used scientific methods to test and prove that there are indeed meridian systems in human beings, various animals and plants. This discovery was later applied to traditional Chinese acupuncture and moxibustion therapy with the accuracy of acupoints, for the treatment of emphysema, pulmonary heart disease, Parkinson's syndrome and other diseases, leading to good results.

1990

1月，我国"七五"期间重大科技攻关项目——新型乙烯裂解炉在辽阳石油化纤公司通过国家级技术鉴定

In January, a new type of ethylene cracker, a major scientific and technological project during the 7th Five-Year Plan, passed national technical appraisal in the Liaoyang Petrochemical Fiber Company.

1991 12月，内地第一座自行设计建造的核电站——浙江秦山核电站首次并网发电。它的建成，结束了内地无核电的历史
The Qinshan Nuclear Power Station in Zhejiang Province, the first self-designed nuclear power plant on the Chinese mainland, was connected to the power grid for the first time in December. Thus, nuclear power using Chinese technology is now part of the mainland generating network.

1992　11月，每秒运行十亿次的巨型计算机——"银河二号"巨型计算机研制成功

The galaxy Type II Supercomputer, capable of calculating one billion bytes of information per second, was developed in November.

1993 11月，一种先进的提炼黄金新工艺及连续提金装置在吉林长春通过了中国科学院组织的鉴定

In November, an advanced new gold extraction process and continuous gold extraction device passed an appraisal organized by the Chinese Academy of Sciences in Changchun, Jilin Province.

科技 Science and Technology

1994 6月，中国第一座引进外国资金、先进设备和技术建设的大型核电站，也是中国第一座大型商业核电站——广东大亚湾核电站正式投入商业运行

The Daya Bay Nuclear Power Station in Guangdong Province, China's first large-scale commercial nuclear power plant built with foreign funds, and foreign advanced equipment and technology, officially began commercial operation in June.

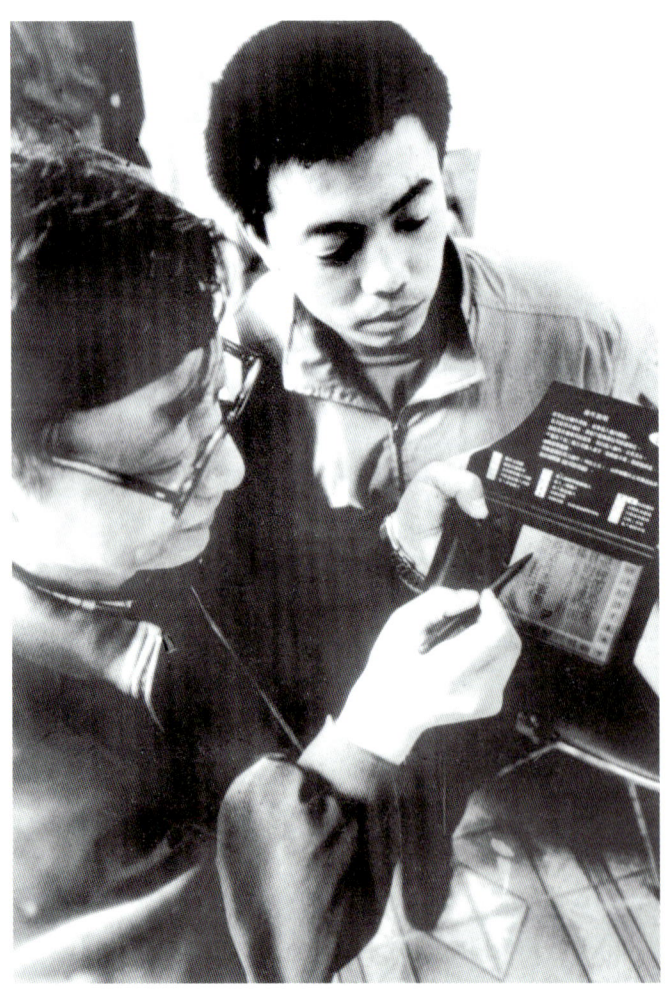

1995 / 世界上第一台"中文掌上型笔输入电脑"在哈尔滨问世
The world's first Chinese palmtop pen input computer has been developed in Harbin in Northeast China.

1996　西安交大科研团队完成的"863计划"项目和课题"JZR—V精密装配机器人视觉系统",是专为国家计划项目"精密一号装配机器人"提供一套完整实用的、具有国际先进水平的视觉系统产品的高科技课题

The JZR-V high-precision assembly robot vision system is a project of the "863 Project" completed by a scientific research team of Xi'an Jiaotong University. It is designed to provide a set of complete and practical vision system products of international advanced level for the State-planned project "Precision Assembly Robot No.1".

1997 南京大学化学化工学院研制成功的能使煤粉和水充分混合变成水煤浆的高效水煤浆添加剂投入规模生产,全年创产值一千七百万元。全国范围内出现了许多科技助力经济发展的模范和典型

The high-efficiency compound CWS, which can fully mix pulverized coal and water into CWS, has been developed by the College of Chemistry and Chemical Engineering of Nanjing University. It has been put into production with an annual output value of 17 million Yuan. This is one of many models that have emerged in boosting economic development across the country.

1998 帕米尔高原，新疆塔什库尔干塔吉克县首次在海拔三千四百至三千六百米的高原种植的两千亩地膜小麦全面成熟并获高产，改写了我国小麦生长最高海拔三千至三千二百米的记录

Some 133 hectares of wheat planted at altitudes of 3,400-3,600 meters in Tashkurgan Tajik County, Xinjiang, on the Pamir Plateau, has fully matured and yielded high yields. This puts an end to the history in which no wheat could be grown in any area with an altitude higher than 3,000-3,200 meters.

1999 亚洲最大的粮食码头——大连北良散粮码头装备了部分具有国际先进水平的国产散粮装卸输送设备

The Dalian Beiliang Bulk Grain Terminal, largest of its kind in Asia, has been equipped with China-made bulk grain handling and conveying equipment of an internationally advanced level.

2000 / 10月，西昌卫星发射中心，中国自行研制的第一颗导航定位卫星——"北斗导航试验卫星"发射升空，顺利进入预定轨道

In October, the Beidou Navigation Experimental Satellite, China's first self-developed navigation and positioning satellite, was launched into orbit from the Xichang Satellite Launch Center, successfully achieving its predetermined orbit.

2001 中国首项移动 B2B（商业对商业）电子商贸服务系统在香港启动
China's first mobile B2B (business to business) e-commerce service system was launched in Hong Kong.

2002 7月，黄河小浪底水库，当时世界水利史上最大规模的一次调水调沙原型人工试验开始进行

In July, China started to conduct a prototype of water and sediment regulation in the history of water conservancy in the world at the Xiaolangdi Reservoir on the Yellow River.

2003

10月,酒泉卫星发射中心,在航天员公寓问天阁里,航天员出征仪式隆重举行,这是全副武装准备出征的我国首位航天员杨利伟

An astronaut journey ceremony was held at the astronaut apartment inquiry pavilion of the Jiuquan Satellite Launch Center in Gansu Province. Yang Liwei, China's first astronaut is seen readying to join the launch project.

2004 5月，北京，第七届科技博览会，中星微电子公司生产的占据全球市场份额最大的多媒体芯片在"中国芯"展台亮相。2003年，由中星微电子公司生产的拥有自主知识产权的"中国芯"第一次成功地打入国际市场，彻底结束了"中国无芯"历史

A shot of the China Core exhibition booth at the 7th Science and Technology Exposition held in Beijing in May: On view is China Core that has achieved the largest share of the world's multimedia chip sector. It was developed by the Beijing Vimicro Electronics Co. Ltd. with its own independent intellectual property rights. China Core was first exported to the international market in 2003, ending a history in which China had no multimedia chips.

2005 4月，中国大陆科学钻探工程竣工典礼在江苏省东海县举行。经过近四年努力，中国大陆科学钻探工程"科钻一井"在江苏省东海县毛北村成功深入地下5158米，并在此基础上取得了一系列科研成果，标志着我国"入地"计划获得重大突破

A ceremony held in Donghai County, Jiangsu Province marked completion of the Chinese Continental Scientific Drilling Project. After nearly four years of efforts, the China Continental Scientific Drilling Project's deep well CCSD-1 successfully penetrated 5,158 meters underground in Maobei Village, Donghai County, Jiangsu Province. On this basis, a series of scientific research achievements have been made, marking a major breakthrough in China's "land entry" program.

2006 / 5月20日,三峡工地雨后初晴,全线浇筑到顶的三峡大坝展现新姿。它是当今世界最大的水利发电工程——三峡水电站的主体工程

On May 20, a fine day marked a return of workers to the construction site of the Three Gorges Project after rain. The Dam's cement work was completed as a major part of the largest hydropower project in the world today.

2007 / 5月,翼龙无人机完成首飞。翼龙无人机是由中航工业成都飞机设计研究所研制的一种中低空、军民两用、长航时多用途无人机。装配一台一百马力活塞发动机,具备全自主平台,是中国无人机制造领域的"当家明星"

China's Pterosaur UAV completed its first maiden flight in May. Pterosaur UAV is a kind of mid-low altitude, dual-purpose flight vehicle for military and civilian use, long-endurance multi-purpose UAV developed by Chengdu Aircraft Design and Research Institute of the Aviation Industry Corp. It is equipped with a 100-horsepower piston engine with full automatic leveling. It is a star of China's UAV manufacturing.

2008 / 9月，华为 WCDMA/HSPA 已在全球获得一百二十一个商用客户，统计数据表明，全球超过半数的 WCDMA/HSPA 运营商选择了华为。2008 年，华为在移动设备市场领域排名全球第三

By September, Huawei WCDMA/HSPA had acquired a total of 121 commercial customers worldwide. Statistics show that more than half of the WCDMA/HSPA operators worldwide chose Huawei. In 2008, Huawei ranked third in the mobile device market.

2009 / 我国发放三张第三代移动通信经营牌照
China has issued three third-generation mobile communication licenses.

2010 / 3月18日，我国自主研制生产的AC313大型民用直升机在江西景德镇首飞成功。这是中国自主研制的首架大型民用直升机，也是亚洲最大的民用直升机

On March 18, the AC313 large civil helicopter, developed and manufactured independently in China, flew successfully for the first time in Jingdezhen, Jiangxi Province. This is the largest of its kind in Asia.

2011 / 7月26日，东太平洋蔚蓝海域，"蛟龙号"载人潜水器成功下潜至5057米。这个下潜深度意味着"蛟龙号"可到达全球超过70%的海底

On July 26, the Jiaolong manned submersible successfully descended to 5,057 meters in the blue waters of the Eastern Pacific Ocean. This means Jiaolong can reach more than 70% of the world's sea floors.

2012 / 10月14日，中国第一艘航空母舰"辽宁舰"在海上试航
China's first aircraft carrier Liaoning undergoes sea trials on October 14.

2013　12月14日21时11分,"嫦娥三号"稳稳地"站"上月面。这是中国探测器首次登上地外天体,中国成为世界上第三个实现月面软着陆的国家

At 21:11 on December 14, Chang'e III stood proudly on the Moon. This is the first time a Chinese probe has landed on an extraterrestrial object. China thus became the third country in the world to achieve a soft landing on the Moon.

2014 / 11月19日，浙江乌镇，为期三天的首届世界互联网大会在这里开幕。这是中国举办的规模最大、层次最高的互联网大会，也是世界互联网领域的高峰会议

On November 19, the First World Internet Conference was held for three days in Wuzhen Town, Zhejiang Province. That is the largest and highest-level Internet conference ever held by China, and also the summit of the world Internet field.

2015 瑞典卡罗琳医学院将诺贝尔生理学或医学奖授予屠呦呦、威廉·坎贝尔和大村智。中国药学家屠呦呦作为青蒿素的主要发现者成为首位获得此奖项的华人科学家

The Karolinska Institute of Sweden awarded the Nobel Prize in Physiology or Medicine to Tu Youyou, William C. Campbell and Satoshi Omura. As the main discoverer of artemisinin, Chinese pharmacist Tu became the first Chinese scientist to win the award.

2016

6月27日,被誉为"中国天眼"的五百米口径球面射电望远镜(FAST),在满天繁星下呈现出的美丽景观。FAST具有中国独立自主知识产权,是世界最大单口径、最灵敏的射电望远镜

The 500-meter-caliber spherical radio telescope (FAST), known as the China's Sky Eye, presented a beautiful view of the star-dotted skies on June 27. FAST is the world's largest single-aperture and most sensitive radio telescope with China's independent intellectual property rights.

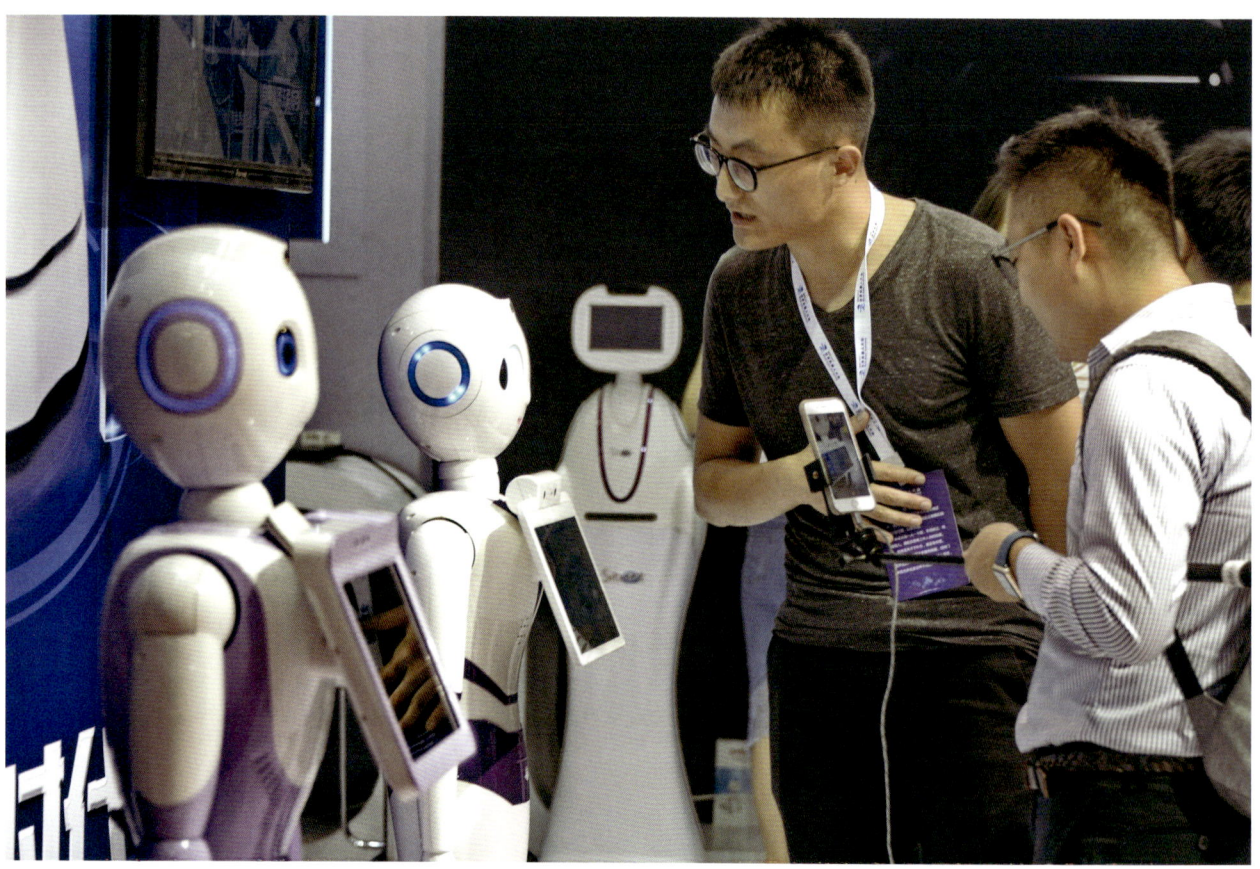

2017

9月22日,北京,世界机器人大会上展出的科大讯飞多用途智能机器人。科大讯飞作为中国最大的智能语音技术提供商,在智能语音技术领域有着长期的研究积累,并在中文语音合成、语音识别、口语评测等多项技术上拥有国际领先的成果

The World Robot Conference held in Beijing on September 22 displayed iFLYTEK a multi-purpose intelligent robot. As the largest supplier of intelligent speech technology in China, iFLYTEK has a long-term research and accumulation experience in the field of intelligent speech technology, and has a leading international achievement in Chinese speech synthesis, speech recognition, spoken language assessment and other technologies.

2018 / 1月，克隆猴"中中"和"华华"在中科院神经科学研究所非人灵长类平台育婴室恒温箱里。体细胞克隆猴的成功，标志着中国在非人灵长类疾病动物模型研究中处于国际领先地位

In January, the cloned monkeys Zhongzhong and Huahua in an incubator of the non-human primate platform nursery in the Institute of Neuroscience of the Chinese Academy of Sciences. The success of somatic cell cloning of monkeys marks the establishment of China's leading position in the study of animal models of non-human primate diseases.

图片提供：
FOTOE、人民画报社、视觉中国、中国图片社、中国新闻社

艾尼瓦尔、安哥、安世明、安佑忠、蔡增乐、曹精义、曹松龄、查春明、常津生、陈飞、陈海宁、陈宏、陈健、陈凯星、陈思禹、陈文、陈燮、陈学思、丁峻、董芳、董荣贵、杜华举、杜泽泉、段崴、凡军、方学辉、傅振欣、高弘杰、高学余、郭大岳、郭建设、韩晓华、贺终荣、胡海昕、黄峰、黄鉴秋、黄禄奎、黄天色、黄一鸣、贾天勇、蒋铎、姜恩宇、蒋林、金立旺、金少月、鞠焕宗、鞠鹏、觉果、赖海隆、李长捷、李春生、李芳、李刚、李红佳、李健、李江松、李开远、李明放、李树贵、李唐、李欣、李远修、梁永强、廖攀、林敬东、刘潺、刘恩泰、刘长新、刘海、刘君凤、刘军喜、刘前刚、刘文敏、刘心宁、刘续、刘宇、柳中央、龙启云、马窦、马厚义、马培文、毛思倩、蒙调元、纳一、潘家珉、庞伟良、庞兴雷、裴鑫、彭振戈、浦超、钱荣摄、邱海鹰、任珑、茹遂初、沈桥、史金明、宋连峰、孙参、孙忠靖、陶明、仝江、土登、王爱青、王福春、王鹏、王绍业、王颂摄、王文澜、王小川、武纯展、吴芳、巫嘉都、吴芒子、吴祖政、肖方、萧云集、解海龙、谢伟民、邢广利、许丛军、徐义根、薛东梅、薛玉斌、杨秉政、杨俊江、杨磊、杨溥涛、杨武敏、杨云倩、杨宗友、殷立勤、荫曾、于文国、袁兆义、张长江、张畅、张晨霖、张春明、张福来、张国俊、张建成、张刘仁、张宁、张平、张申生、张生贵、张晓华、张旭、张肆文、赵明清、赵琬微、赵众志、郑书福、郑永吉、钟欣、周国强、周家志、竺钢、朱广智、朱宪民、壮锦、邹宪、邹毅

（按姓氏拼音排序）

Photos contributed by FOTOE, CFB, VCG, CNS, CIG

Photos courtesy of Ai Niwar, An Ge, An shiming, An Youzhong, Cai Zengle, Cao Jingyi, Cao Songling, Cha Chunming, Chang Jinsheng, Chen Fei, Chen Haining, Chen Hong, Chen Jian, Chen Kaixing, Chen Siyu, Chen Wen, Chen Xie, Chen Xuesi, Ding Jun, Dong Fang, Dong Ronggui, Du Huaju, Du Zequan, Duan Wei, Fan Jun, Fang Xuehui, Fu Zhenxin, Gao Hongjie, Gao Xueyu, Guo Dayue, Guo Jianshe, Han Xiaohua, He Zhongrong, Hu Haixin, Huang Feng, Huang Jianqiu, Huang Lukui, Huang Tianse, Huang Yiming, Jia Tianyong, Jiang Duo, Jiang Enyu, Jiang Lin, Jin Liwang, Jin Shaoyue, Ju Huanzhong, Ju Peng, Jue Guo, Lai Hailong, Li Changjie, Li Chunsheng, Li Fang, Li Gang, Li Hongjia, Li Jian, Li Jiangsong, Li Kaiyuan, Li Mingfang, Li Shugui, Li Tang, Li Xin, Li Yuanxiu, Liang Yongqiang, Liao Pan, Lin Jingdong, Liu Chan, Liu Entai, Liu Changxin, Liu Hai, Liu Junfeng, Liu Junxi, Liu Qiangang, Liu Wenmin, Liu Xinning, Liu Xu, Liu Yu, Liu Zhongyang, Long Qiyun, Ma Dou, Ma Houyi, Ma Peiwen, Mao Siqian, Meng Tiaoyuan, Na Yi, Pan Jiamin, Pang Weiliang, Pang Xinglei, Pei Xin, Peng Zhenge, Pu Chao, Qian Rongshe, Qiu Haiying, Ren Long, Rui Suchu, Shen Qiao, Shi Jinming, Song Lianfeng, Sun Shen, Sun Zhongjing, Tao Ming, Tong Jiang, Tu Deng, Wang Aiqing, Wang Fuchun, Wang Peng, Wang Shaoye, Wang Songshen, Wang Wenlan, Wang Xiaochuan, Wu Chunzhan, Wu Fang, Wu Jiadu, Wu Mangzi, Wu Zuzheng, Xiao Fang, Xiao Yunji, Xie Hailong, Xie Weimin, Xing Guangli, Xu Congjun, Xu Yigen, Xue Dongmei, Xue Yubin, Yang Bingzheng, Yang Junjiang, Yang Lei, Yang Putao, Yang Wumin, Yang Yunqian, Yang Zongyou, Yin Liqin, Yin Zeng, Yu Wenguo, Yuan Zhaoyi, Zhang Changjiang, Zhang Chang, Zhang Chenlin, Zhang Chunming, Zhang Fulai, Zhang Guojun, Zhang Jiancheng, Zhang Liu Ren, Zhang Ning, Zhang Ping, Zhang Shensheng, Zhang Shenggui, Zhang Xiaohua, Zhang Xu, Zhang Yiwen, Zhao Mingqing, Zhao Wanwei, Zhao Zhongzhi, Zheng Shufu, Zheng Yongji, Zhong Xin, Zhou Guoqiang, Zhou Jiazhi, Zhu Gang, Zhu Guangzhi, Zhu Xianmin, Zhuang Jin, Zou Xian, Zou Yi

(Arranged in alphabetical order of surnames)